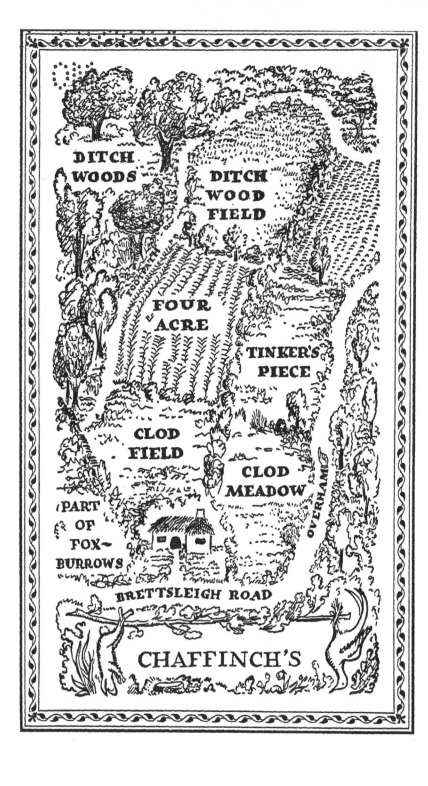

HIS
OWN
PLACE

by

H. W. Freeman

TYPOGRAPHY BY FRANK J. LIEBERMAN
PRINTED IN THE UNITED STATES OF AMERICA
BY QUINN & BODEN COMPANY, INC., RAHWAY, N. J.

HIS
OWN
PLACE

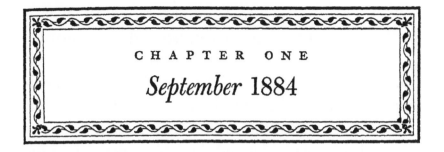

CHAPTER ONE

September 1884

JOSS ELVIN BENT OVER HIS COPYBOOK, BREATHING HARD, his tongue out, his pen scratching.

"Honesty is the best policy," he wrote. "Honesty is the best policy. Honesty is the best policy."

He wrote it three times in the blank space provided and then sat back to rest his cramped fingers before going on to "Necessity is the mother of invention." It was a warm September morning and his forehead sweated with the effort of concentration; but his third essay was no less a caricature of the suavely curving copperplate than his first. Then, while he was still absorbing this unfortunate truth, a small black fly settled on his second "Honesty," he made a dash with his fist, and smudged the whole page. He felt his face go stiff with disgust, he felt most uncomfortable, he felt hollow inside; and there was still a quarter of an hour to go before dinner-time. He had had enough.

"If you please, teacher," he said, poking up a hand.

"Well, Elvin?" said Mr. Deeks, looking up from a heap of arithmetic exercises.

"If you please, sir, can I leave the room?"

"Have you been taking medicine?" said Mr. Deeks, always suspicious of such a request.

3

"Yes, sir," said Joss, cool and unfaltering, although it was a lie; but it was an ancient, licensed and venial lie.

Mr. Deeks, too, was aware of this lie; but since on occasion boys had been really known to have taken medicine, he yielded to the authority of the word and nodded.

Joss trotted out of the classroom on noisy hobnails. A passage led to the lobby and the lobby opened into the school yard, into the freedom and the fresh air that he thought he wanted; but when he reached the lobby door, he no longer wanted them, for there, on a row of hooks, hung the various bags and satchels of the boys who had brought their dinner. This morning Joss had had one small slice of dry bread for breakfast and a cup of weak tea.

"Now do you run along to school," his mother had said, " 'cause I hain't got nothen to give you for your dinner. 'Haps for tea there'll be a bit of suthun."

So Joss had run along to school, and now he was hungry. That was what was the matter with him, that was why his smudged copybook had caused him such distress, and the sight of all those bags and satchels made him feel as empty as he actually was. He tiptoed up to them and gazed. Then with timid reverence he undid one and looked inside. It contained bread and cheese, a slice of cold baked pudding and an apple. This was food, real food, he could not but treat it reverently. He did up the satchel again and tried another. Here he found bread and butter, a slice of cold bacon and two currant buns. Some folks were lucky. But some were luckier still, for the next satchel yielded a packet of sandwiches

4

and inside them was a thick layer of the juiciest, the most fragrant, potted meat. He knew that satchel well. It was a capacious, well-filled one and belonged to Edgar Clary, whose father was a farmer; there was always plenty of food on a farm.

For a minute or so Joss stared at the sandwiches and his mouth watered till he could bear it no longer. Honesty, he knew, was the best policy—he had just written it out three times; but would young Clary notice if he ate just one? It took him several hesitating moments to get the sandwich to his lips; but when he did, it vanished in next to no time at all. After that his hunger, like a fed flame, rose up and took possession. Honesty, discretion and restraint went to the winds and he ate greedily, without stopping, till he reached the last one. Once again he hesitated, and then—in for a penny, in for a pound—he ate that too. The packet was empty and he guiltily brushed the crumbs off his threadbare corduroy jacket. He knew he had done wrong, he was a thief; but there was something solid in his stomach now, it was hard to feel sorry.

What troubled him more was how to avoid the consequences of his crime. Edgar Clary was twelve, a year older than he was, he was several inches taller, and even at the best of times he was not over-gentle with boys smaller than himself. He would miss his sandwiches and naturally suspect the one boy who had "left the room" during the last lesson—the more so because every one in the parish knew that Joss never had enough to eat. All the same, no one could prove it—he brushed a last crumb off his sleeve and carefully did up the satchel—there was no evidence against him, and he would never, never do such a thing again; he was not a thief. Reassured by his hopes and the certainty of his future good behaviour, he crept demurely back to the classroom and achieved three quite passable versions of "Necessity is the mother of invention" before Mr. Deeks ordered the monitor to sound the dinner-hour bell.

Joss's desk was near the door and as soon as the bell rang, he took advantage of it. Before any of his schoolmates had reached their satchels, he was in the yard, and five minutes later he was on all fours in the back of the vicarage garden, groping in the nettles for windfalls. He ate them at his leisure, reclining on a bed of dry leaves in a ditch, and they went down very well after the potted meat. Then, after he had combed two meadows in vain search for mushrooms, the school bell set up its unfriendly clang and he hurried back.

He reached the yard just as the boys were forming up, and took his place at the end of the line. No one paid any special attention to him, not even Edgar Clary, and later on, when he allowed himself one or two judicious peeps over his shoulder, Edgar's face was steadfastly bent to his Bible. Joss settled back complacently in his hard wooden desk and gave himself up to the parable of the Good Shepherd. It was so mysterious and unintelligible to him that he was even a little frightened by it, but he had no difficulty in learning it off by heart. Indeed, he was the first child in the class to repeat it without a mistake, and, as a mark of praise, was allowed to read where he liked in his Bible for the rest of the hour. How different life was on a full belly! Even the Wars of the Roses could be interesting—

But good things come to an end. Mr. Deeks looked at the clock and shuffled his feet.

"Stand," he commanded. "Hands together."

"Our Father wh'chart in heaven—" The conjoint murmur rose on the air like a rustle of leaves, and with half-shut eyes Joss ventured another peep over his shoulder. But he hastily turned his head round again, for this time Edgar was looking at him. He was staring at him over his clasped hands with his eyes wide open and his chin sticking out.

"For Thine is the kingdom, the power and the glory, for ever and ever, amen." As if a wind had suddenly dropped, the rustle came to an abrupt end. Mr. Deeks nodded, the monitor rang the bell, and there was a rush to the door. Joss was the first out of it, and if only he cleared the yard with sufficient start, he could plunge through the hedges to safety. But his legs were not long enough, and as he came out on the road in front of the school gate, Edgar was already close behind. There was no mistaking his intentions. He threw his empty satchel away, he stretched out an arm and made a grab. He missed by an inch, grabbed again, and had Joss by the shoulder. But before he could tighten his grip, Joss turned suddenly and ducked forward under his arm, only to be caught by the slack of his jacket, as Edgar swung round with his other arm outstretched. Now he had got him, he thought, but Joss spun round on his

7

heel and the smooth corduroy slipped out of Edgar's fingers. Half the school were standing round them watching; they knew some of Joss's tricks and waited eagerly for more.

"Hold him tight, Edgar," shouted one of them mockingly. "He's an eel, he is."

But Joss was tired of being an eel. He knew he could not keep it up much longer against Edgar's size and strength, and made for the hedge-bank. Here, in front of him, there was a pair of tall elm-trees, their trunks well apart, but their topmost boughs entwined. One of them sent a sloping limb down over the bank, and for any who knew how to use it, this was a short cut into the body of the tree. Joss took the short cut. He gave a jump and caught two handfuls of twigs, and without a pause he went up hand over hand till he could get his feet on the limb. After that he just swarmed up it like a sailor on a rope, till his head touched the main trunk. Then, crooking a knee between his two arms, he swung himself upright on the branch and looked down, grinning.

"Goo on, Edgar," mocked the children, delighted by this free show of acrobatics. "You can't catch him now."

Edgar knew that he could not. He knew that Joss was king in this country. To be sure, he could have waited; some time or other Joss would have had to come down. But the gibes of his schoolmates exasperated and humiliated him; and he was one who wanted his own way even when he knew he could not have it.

"I'll larn you," he shouted. "I'll larn you to steal my dinner."

"How d'you know I stole it?" Joss shouted back.

" 'Cause I knew you didn't go home to dinner to-day," shouted Edgar. "You hain't got no dinner to go to. I'll larn you."

"All right, come on and larn me," tittered Joss.

For a time he had been sorry for what he had done, and if Edgar had given him a chance to explain—though he had known all along that Edgar would do no such thing—he would have gone on being sorry. But now he was just a weaker animal pursued by a stronger; he was just striving to best his natural enemy and he gloried in it, for he was safe now, or soon would be.

Immediately above him, between his branch and the next, was a considerable length of bare trunk; but there was a way up. You raised your right foot and edged it round the trunk till it found the stump of a branch, long since fallen. Then, hanging on to the furrowed elm-bark with your finger-tips, you raised your whole weight on that stump and sought for another, similar one, a little higher up, with your left foot. Having found that, you raised yourself on it, and there was the next branch, ready to your hand. It was a bit of a stretch for Joss's short legs; but he had little weight to lift and was proof against all fear of height; it was just like going upstairs for him. One, two, three, and his hand was on the branch; he hauled himself up on it, squatted astride, and still grinning, peered down to see what was happening below him.

9

Edgar had not been equal to the short cut, but he was clambering steadily up the trunk by way of the lower branches. Already Joss could see his hands on the branch below his own, and a minute later he stood with both his feet on it, looking doubtfully up at the intimidating bare patch. Joss retired one branch higher up, to be right out of harm's way, and wondered what Edgar would do.

"Come on, bor," he shouted. "Come and larn me to climb."

The taunt resolved Edgar's doubts. He flung his arms round the trunk and thrust out his right foot for the first stump. He got it, poised his weight on it, and thrusting out for the other stump, got that too. He paused, triumphantly, to rest—Joss was not the only one who knew how to climb. But then what Joss had expected happened. Not content with looking at the elm-bark in front of him, he turned his head sideways and saw the void beyond and below. That was the last of his little triumph. His inside went all loose, his muscles went flabby; the branch above him was leagues away, and now so was the one below; and all that stood between him and annihilation was a couple of sere stumps. He could move neither up nor down, and dug his fingers into the bark with despairing violence. To complete his agony, a thin, hot stream of liquid suddenly struck him between the eyes and he could no longer see; but he could hear the throng below, the boys and girls jeering and guffawing at him, having the time of their lives. Surely death could not be worse than this—

The little stream soon pattered off to its natural end, but to Edgar it seemed like the end of a deluge. He could open his eyes and see the light, he had one affliction the less, and he was still alive. Clutching the trunk with all the strength of his arms, he reached down cautiously with his foot and felt for the branch. If he ever got to the ground again, Joss could have his dinner every day; all he wanted was to be alive. Yes, he had got the branch, his foot was firmly braced on it, he was saved—

Joss knew nothing of these charitable resolves, but he did know that Edgar was now within measurable distance of the ground, and if he himself was to get there first, he must hurry. He climbed on a little higher up the trunk, crawled out along a lateral branch, and stepped neatly into the top of the neighboring tree. Edgar was still halfway up the other, resting after his fright, when he dropped to the ground again.

"Hey, Edgar," he called derisively, "I'll larn you." Then he darted off through the opposite hedge and made for home; he wanted his tea.

It was not much of a home, the Elvins' two-roomed cottage. The clay cob of which it was built was crumbling away; the whitewash was peeling off; the thatch, torn to tatters by the sparrows, let in daylight. Inside, the furniture, so often familiarly described as "sticks," could have received no apter name. A leaf-table with one leaf, two Windsor chairs without backs, a corner cupboard without a door, a horsehair sofa on three legs and a wooden bed with no legs at all—there was hardly a piece but looked as if it had already been to the chopping-block. But it was all quite clean, as clean as was possible, that is, with a stamped earth floor and no mats, and it had need be, for all available space in the room was taken up with damp clothes airing.

Joss's mother was stirring a saucepan over a fire of twigs when he entered. She was a little woman with no definite features, toothless and sunken-cheeked. She wore a black dress, green with age and so voluminously skirted that she looked even thinner and frailer in it than she actually was. Faith Elvin had been born in the "hungry forties" and had never had the chance to grow fat.

"Hullo, Joss, you're late," she said, more for the sake of something to say than because it mattered. "Come on, boy, let's sit down and have we teas. I'm hungry."

"What have you got there, Mother?" said Joss, perching himself on one of the backless chairs and looking mistrustfully at the saucepan; it smelt mainly of steam.

"Father brought back a swede this arternoon," she said, sprinkling a little salt in the saucepan. "He wouldn't wait for me to cook that. He had a piece raw and went off to The Rose—to see if he could earn a shilling," she added with a sniff.

Joss was silent. He had had a lot of swede lately.

"I know that ain't much," she went on apologetically, "but that'll fill your belly. Come on now, sit up to the table like a good boy." She brought the saucepan to the table and shook out a steamy orange sludge on their two cracked plates.

Joss poked at his share with a coarse iron spoon and

tasted a mouthful, but somehow or other he could not swallow it; he was sick of the stuff.

"Hey, what's the matter?" his mother scolded. "Ain't that good enow?"

Joss pushed his plate away. "I can't eat that," he said.

"Did you get anything for dinner?" said his mother, a little anxiously.

Joss nodded. "Somebody gave me a bit of bread and paste," he said, lying; she would not like to hear he had stolen it.

"I'm glad, pore brat," she said, eyeing him kindly. "You wholly need that— Hey, where are you off to?"

"Oh, just down the lane," said Joss offhand, as he unlatched the door. "Arter some mushrooms, 'haps."

"Well, don't be late agin," she said reprovingly. "Do, there 'on't be no supper left."

Once outside, Joss did not waste any time looking for mushrooms, but took a straight line across the fields to the Overham road. He could not let his mother know that for fear of being kept in, but as soon as she had told him his father was at The Rose, his mind was made up. That was the real reason why he could not touch his plate of boiled swede. Matthew Elvin, his father, had a fascination for Joss, and above all when he was at The Rose.

Matthew's father, like most of his forefathers back to the Middle Ages, had farmed his own land in the village common field and grazed his own cattle on the village common grazing; he had been a peasant. But halfway through his life the Enclosure Act had deprived him of his land and turned him and his sons into farm labourers. To the world at large this was now just history, something done in the interests of society; but to Matthew and his father it had been misery, and society had treated them abominably. It had not only robbed and degraded them. It had made them slave for wages that would not support life and then thrown them on the rates to keep them alive. It had reviled them as paupers, starved them, pulled down their houses and lodged them in barns and stables, driven them to work in gangs. By now, in Matthew's time, things were getting better. A man could manage to live on his wages without being forced on the rates; but there was not always work to be had, and Matthew's strength had suffered from his earlier privations. He could not always do the work required of him and farmers grew shy of employing him. He had to fall back on casual labour and when that failed, on the "parish." It was not to be wondered at that Joss was the last surviving member of a family of seven.

Trouble and want had completely conquered Faith Elvin; they had washed her out and left her colourless. Not so with Matthew. His body might have been subdued, but he stubbornly refused to deliver up his lively spirit. Dark hours he certainly had; but he still contrived, whenever possible, to enjoy life. In this respect there was still much of the child in him, and it was this that endeared him to Joss. When he was without work or without money, he did not stop at home, like his wife, and brood. He went out to see what he could do, or at least to see what he could see. The things he did were seldom

14

profitable and often trivial. He would spend hours making fancy walking-sticks for Joss and his friends, or little rush cages with pebble birds inside. He would tramp miles to find the right piece of wood for a potato-dibber, and sometimes he brought back a swede or a turnip, or on lucky days a rabbit. But from all these things he got a great deal of pleasure, as Joss found whenever he went out with him. "Air is free," he used to say, "and there's all the world to look at."

It was natural, too, that such a man should love company, and seldom a day passed but he went down to The Rose at some time or other in search of it. He hardly ever had anything to spend, but there were ways and means of getting the price of a drink. There was the occasional charity of the kind-hearted; there were games such as bowls or "ringing the bull," at which he was an adept; and there was his one accomplishment. Matthew was a singer. He had no voice to speak of and he could not read a note of music—in fact he could hardly read his own name; but he only had to hear a song once to pick up the tune, and no string of verses was too long for him to remember. Ever since he had been old enough to go to a public house, he had been listening to songs and storing them up in his memory. He knew soldier songs and sailor songs, bawdy songs and religious songs, love songs, comic songs, eighteenth-century and Victorian ballads off the broadsheets, and a few folksongs that had come down direct from his Tudor ancestors. He had all the tunes pat, and although they were often very flowery and complicated, he never scamped a note, just as he never forgot a word. He sang partly for the pure pleasure of it, but singing was also in demand at The Rose. Village people and passing strangers in those days liked a good song with a good tune to it. They listened attentively, they made comments and applauded when it was finished, and they often stood the singer a drink. Sometimes they gave him money instead, and that was what Matthew's wife had meant by "earning a shilling at The Rose." But very little of it ever found its way to her, and being not unnaturally jealous of pleasures she could not share, she pretended to disapprove of his goings-on "at the beer-shop." She had never guessed that for Joss they were the principal part of his father's fascination.

The point where he joined the Overham road was opposite a small, broken-down wicket-gate in a high hedge, and at the sight of it he shouted and skipped with excitement. It was only a mile to The Rose now, and for something to be going on with, here he was at old Chaffinch's.

He skipped across to the gate and peered through it into the garden beyond, or what had once been a garden, it was now so overgrown and neglected. Behind it stood a lath-and-plaster cottage that showed every sign, not only of similar neglect, but of deliberate maltreatment as well. The front door was open and half off its hinges, there were great holes and cracks in the plaster walls, the downstairs windows were boarded up with old packing-cases, and upstairs there was no longer a scrap of glass to be seen, except for a single small triangle almost hidden under falling thatch from the eaves. It did not escape Joss's eye, however, and as soon as he espied it, he picked up a stone and let fly. There was a sharp dry tinkle as the glass fell in shivers on the bedroom floor, and the moment after an odd figure of a man came running out of the open door. He was a little, under-sized man with a monkeyish face and tufty grey whiskers; his hair hung in greasy locks down his neck and his only visible clothing consisted of two sacks, one slung round his waist and the other over his shoulders. He ran halfway down the garden path, and then stopped short, to shake his fist and scream inarticulate curses at the top of his voice. That was what Joss had been waiting for.

He knew nothing about old Chaffinch, except that he was crazy and lived there in unspeakable filth and poverty; but though he was quite harmlessly crazy, that was enough for the village urchins, who, just for the pleasure of seeing him like this, with his sacks and flying locks, screaming and shaking his fist, had smashed every pane of glass in his house, had broken down his door and gate, had pelted holes in his plaster. Joss enjoyed it as much as any of them, but this time there was still better fun to come, so after one good look at the old monkey-face, he skipped happily along.

It was getting towards dusk when he reached The Rose, and already lamps shone bright in the windows. The curtains, however, were not yet drawn and Joss could see from the number of heads that the taproom was fairly full. That was how he liked it. What was even better, his father was at this moment singing and

Joss knew the song he was singing. It was *The Young Sailor Cut Down in His Prime*, one of his favourites. Joss had never quite understood why, just by spending his money on women, the young sailor should have met with this fate, but he always enjoyed the vigorous celebrations at his funeral, which formed the chorus:

So we will beat the drums over him and play the fifes
    merrily,
Play the dead march as we carry him along.
We will take him to the churchyard and fire three vol-
    leys over him,
For he was a young sailor cut down in his prime.

Joss liked it so much that while he stood there with his face pressed against the window, he joined in, and when, at the last chorus, the applause came and some one filled up his father's mug, he applauded too. It was after that, when the window was no longer so enthralling, that he noticed some one standing behind him and looking over his head. He turned his head sharply and saw a uniformed figure in a tall helmet. It was the police constable from Brettsleigh and Joss edged instinctively away from him; policemen never boded good for poor people or little boys. But the policeman was not interested in Joss. He, too, turned from the window and walked up to the inn door; he opened it and strode into the taproom. From outside Joss could feel the sudden hush that fell on the company, and led on by a fearful curiosity, he crept in after him as far as the taproom door. To his horror, the policeman was addressing his father.

"Matthew Elvin," he was saying, "I arrest you in the name of the law, for stealing a swede, the property of Martin Wright, of the Rookery Farm, Brettsleigh. You'd better come without any fuss." He took out a pair of handcuffs.

Joss held his breath, wondering what his father would do. He had once seen him fight a man in the inn yard, a far better man than himself, and knock him senseless. There was nobody like his father. But after a moment's silence Matthew just laughed.

"All right, bor," he said, "let me finish my beer." He emptied his mug and held out his hands. "How long shall I get, bor?"

"Oh, three months, I should reckon," said the policeman, as he slipped on the handcuffs. "You know, mate," he added in a lower voice, "I can't help myself. Owd Wright's on the bench."

"Yes, I know," said Matthew bitterly, addressing the whole room. "They 'on't give us work, they 'on't give us housen, they 'on't let us eat. Why don't they strangle us at birth?"

"Come on, my man, that's enow," said the constable, seizing his elbow.

"All right, constable," said Matthew, and started to follow him across the room, but after a couple of steps he stopped and stared at the door. "Why, blast," he cried, "if that ain't my boy Joss! Come you here, my boy."

Hanging his head with shyness of the public gaze,

Joss obeyed. Matthew bent down and clumsily placed his fettered hands on the boy's shoulder.

"Listen here, my boy," he said. "I want you to do an errand for me. Do you go home to your mother and tell her I've gone to prison for a swede, a swede as I took to fill your belly. But that warn't no good, my boy, and there ain't only one thing I can tell you. You 'on't never fill him till you grow your own."

"Come on now," said the policeman, tugging impatiently at his arm, "we can't stay here all night."

"All right," said Matthew, brushing Joss's cheek with his whiskers and straightening up. "Farewell, boy."

"Farewell, Father." Joss watched him follow the policeman out. He had never felt prouder of his father.

FAITH ELVIN HAD ALWAYS BEEN OF A RELIGIOUS TURN OF
mind, and when Matthew Elvin died of typhus in Ipswich jail, she gave herself up to religion. Matthew was
no great loss to her, but now that he was gone, she felt
she had nothing more to expect from this life; it seemed
high time to prepare for the next. What she had hitherto
regarded as crosses to be borne she now welcomed with
half-exultant resignation as the means to heaven, and
took a pride in her sufferings. She became an assiduous
church-goer and spent long hours on her knees; she read
daily in her Bible and the less she understood it the more
it comforted her; her ordinary conversation was a continual rebuke to human wickedness. Altogether, she was
very disagreeable company for Joss, but now, luckily
for him, he did not have to spend so much of his time
with her; for, despite her piety, the vicar's washing without Matthew's casual earnings was not enough to keep
them both, and Joss, at the age of eleven, had to leave
school and look for work. At the same time it so happened that Walter Clary, Edgar's father, needed a backhouse boy, and Joss was taken on.

His mother was chastely gratified and thanked God
on his behalf.

"I did well to name you arter the great king of Judah," she said. "Your father wanted to call you Edward arter the Prince of Wales, but I said, 'No, Josiah turned to the Lord with all his heart, and with all his soul, and with all his might. My boy is going to be called Josiah.' And now I know I was right."

Joss, however, was not so enthusiastic about his name, and he soon discovered that little boys were wanted on farms because they were cheap.

Walter Clary was sprung from the same peasant stock as Matthew Elvin. His father and Matthew's had gone to the same dame-school together and had grazed their respective cattle on the same village common; but when Matthew's father was turned off his land, Walter's had received, thanks to his wife's good cooking, a happier lot. She had previously been in service at the manor and was such a good cook that after her marriage she was still summoned there on special occasions to take charge of the kitchen. Then, when the peasants' holdings were enclosed and new tenants were required for the new farms created from them, the squire and his lady had not been ungrateful, and her husband had been set up as the first occupant of Foxburrows Farm, where, also, she was still available for the needs of the kitchen. Since that event scarcely a generation had passed, but the Clarys were now no less firmly established in the social order as masters than the Elvins were as "men."

Foxburrows was a six-horse farm of some hundred and fifty acres and Walter Clary farmed it according to the best principles of nineteenth-century mixed husbandry, which by now, the middle eighties, had reached its perfection. A flock of blackface sheep kept his light-ish land stamped firm and it bore heavy crops of corn and roots; there were always cattle in his yards and pigs in his sties; and in general he put back into his land as much as he took from it. Walter Clary was a good farmer and though he lived well in his square red-brick house, he worked hard for it.

Joss, too, was expected to work hard and as the duties of backhouse boy had no definite limit, he worked harder than most. He carried water and chopped wood for the kitchen, he cleaned boots and carried baskets of linen on washing-day; he dug the garden, mixed bait for the cattle, fed the pigs and helped any one round the yards—stockman, horseman or shepherd—who needed help; and when there was nothing left for him to do there, he was sent out into the fields to scare crows, to pull docks, or to mow thistles. For these multifarious labours, which began at five in the morning and often lasted till nine at night, he was paid a shilling a week. It was certainly not a fair wage for the work he did, but it was the customary wage, and surprisingly enough, Joss throve on it. The regular shilling added to his mother's washing money made all the difference, and now, although it was still a struggle for them to make ends meet, he always had enough to eat. His cheeks filled out, his shoulders broadened, and he was so wiry that even a fifteen-hour day at harvest-time did not tire him beyond measure. He had the blood of labouring men in his veins.

Joss himself did not complain. For him the main hardship was the frost that nipped his fingers on winter mornings; but this was a small thing beside the continual excitement of belonging to a farm and being an inside witness of its manifold workings. He saw the stockman ring pigs and deliver calves, he saw the shepherd extract ticks, he saw the horseman build stacks and thatch them. There was always some new operation to watch, some new skill to admire; and Joss's only grievance was that he was only a backhouse boy, and still debarred from doing a man's work.

Three years passed. Joss was fourteen now, a square, sturdy lad, and conscious of the rising strength of his limbs; but while every one else was busy with the autumn sowings, he was still scaring crows off the first winter wheat. He liked that better than chopping wood, mixing hogwash and all his other fiddling jobs about the farmyard. It took him out in the open fields and there he was his own master. He could potter about the hedges looking for birds' nests or setting snares for rabbits, he could have a few breathless moments vainly stalking a hare, and sometimes he had the luck to watch a couple of stoats fighting. There was always something to look at in the hedges, and after he had spent a day or two in a field, he knew almost every tree and bush around it; it was as if they belonged to him. Even the actual work of scaring crows was not without its rewards. He often got tired of the shouting, but he was seldom tired of looking at the sky, for in the sky, too, there was nearly always something to look at. There were clouds to tell the weather by and smoke from field fires and chimneys; there were solitary birds and flocks of birds, and the rooks it was his duty to scare away; there was a great deal to be learnt about rooks. Taking it all together, scaring crows was not a bad job and he could easily have been content with it—if only it had been man's work. That was the humiliating part of it, and what humiliated him still more on this fine October morning was that just over the hedge in the next field, with a plough and a team of horses, breaking up a stubble all by himself, was young Edgar Clary.

Edgar was now fifteen, and while Joss was still held to his petty child's tasks, he was being systematically taught the trade of a farmer, he was doing a man's work and already regarded himself as a man. With so much difference between their respective rôles on the farm, they were not much together, but at the times when they were, Edgar did not attempt, as Joss might have expected, and, indeed, would have preferred, to pay off old scores; he just ignored Joss and gave himself the airs of a man. That was the thing that humiliated Joss, and what made it worse was that he knew in his bones that he could drive that plough just as well as Edgar.

He looked enviously over the low hedge as Edgar drew up to the headland, and it was more than he could stand. He had to do something to make known his feelings.

"Ee-yar-ico," he sang out in his loudest, most liquid voice, "ee-yar-ico-o!"

Edgar brought his horses round on the headland and

25

stopped to breathe them. He knew Joss's scarecrow song well enough, but he also knew that at this moment it was a song of defiance directed at him, and it stung him. Joss might think he had forgotten the old scores, but he had not. He could never forget the theft of those sandwiches—they were his property—he could never forget the indignities he had suffered on that elm-tree, and he was still longing to get his own back. But Joss had lately grown so thick and square, he was not at all sure he could beat him in a straight fight. He looked round him in exasperation.

"Hey, young Joss," he shouted, suddenly pointing, "d'you see that 'aire owd bunch of mistletoe? I dare you to fetch me a bit."

The mistletoe he pointed to hung from the topmost branch of a tall poplar in the hedge between them. It was an old tree, and whether by some weakening of the roots or by pressure of the wind, it had taken a list over the hedge at a perilous angle. As far as halfway up, this list was a positive help to the climber, for branches stood out from the upper face of the trunk like rungs on a ladder. Then, for no apparent reason, the branches suddenly deserted the upper for the under surface, from which they stretched out boldly earthwards. Here the climber had no natural support from the trunk, and both the slope of the branches and gravity were against him, so that he depended entirely on the strength of his handhold, and that not merely for a branch or two, but for a good fifteen foot.

Joss stood still for a moment and ran his eye over the

tree. It was not an easy climb, he could see, but he knew what he could do, and he could just see his way to the top. He turned to Edgar again.

"I'll get you that," he said, scornfully, "but will you go too? I dare you, Edgar."

"What d'you reckon?" replied Edgar with equal scorn. "If you go, I go. But you 'on't do that, my lad."

" 'On't I?" Joss pushed through a gap in the hedge and ran to the foot of the tree. "Do you watch now. You'll wholly need to."

The ladder part was easy enough and he treated it like a ladder; but after that came his first problem, which was to transfer himself from the upper to the under surface of the trunk. His feet were now poised on the last of the upper branches. The first of the under branches was a little higher, though he could touch it with his foot; the next was quite beyond the reach of his hand. Joss paused long enough to get his breath and then clasped the trunk with both arms. They were just long enough to go round it, and getting a good grip, he drew himself up and clasped it with his legs. In this way he hauled himself up a couple of feet, till his head was level with the second under branch. Then, hanging on by his legs, he edged his shoulders round till he got both hands on the branch, took a firm hold, and let his legs swing round the trunk to his foothold on the branch below. He put one arm round the trunk to steady him and paused again.

His next problem was how to clamber up these under branches to the top and it was not going to be pleasant. None of his tricks would help him here, it was just a matter of muscle and grip. Joss spat on his hands, one after the other, and started again. The branches here were closer together, and but for the slope of the trunk, would have been quite good climbing. As it was, Joss felt as if he was climbing upside down, and for once in his life he reached the top of a tree with relief. His head was buzzing and he was glad to hug the trunk for a minute or so to get his breath again. Then, stretching out his hand, he pulled off a sprig of mistletoe, clenched his teeth on it, and began to clamber down. That was not pleasant either, but at least he no longer had his own weight to lift; and then there was the cross-over. This time he had to edge one arm and one leg round the trunk till he got a grip with his thighs. Then a push from his arm on the branch, and he was on the upper slope of the trunk again. Another minute, and he was down on the ground, holding out his sprig of mistletoe.

"There you are," he panted. "Now that's your turn."

Edgar stood by his plough-handles, wavering. His cheeks were a little pale.

"Are you afraid?" said Joss, grinning.

"Afraid? Do you wait," said Edgar, and strode manfully over to the tree.

Any fool could have climbed the first half and Edgar managed it so easily that he began to think he would get to the mistletoe after all. He had taken careful note of Joss's tactics and when he reached the cross-over, he duly hoisted himself out on the trunk. His arms and legs were still substantially longer than Joss's and to his satisfaction he was able to gain the first handhold and foothold after one hoist. Then, slowly and cautiously, he let his body swing round the trunk and took the strain on his hands and feet as Joss had done. But then, too, he looked up and saw all the sloping branches between him and the mistletoe. They promised no real help, for all the way he would be bearing his own weight without chance of a rest, and there was nothing below him—he dared not look down—nothing except the ground. Edgar's courage went from him and he blindly thrust his left leg out to recapture the safety of the trunk. But he was now too frightened to remember all Joss's moves and he could not get a grip, not a grip that he could trust to take him round the trunk again. There was only one thing left to do now and he did it.

"Joss!" he shouted.

"Yes, what is that?" came the answer, from what seemed an immeasurable distance.

"I can't get down," shouted Edgar, and his voice sounded so weak and miserable that he felt ashamed of it.

"All right, I'm a-coming," called Joss, and how assured and comforting his voice sounded! To Edgar it was like an hour, but actually Joss was up at the cross-over and giving him orders in little more than a minute.

"Here, give me that leg," he said, and dragging Edgar's boot round the trunk as far as he could, pinned it with one of his arms. "Now put your left arm round the trunk," he said. "Get that round as fur as you kin, and hold tight. Now pry agin the branch with the other. Pry, bor, pry."

Edgar obeyed, straining hard, and suddenly, with the

29

help of a little push from Joss's free arm, he found himself on the right side of the trunk.

"Now hold tight a tick," said Joss, and slipping off the branch on which he was straddled, he left the way clear for Edgar. "Come on, bor, let yourself slide a foot and you're there."

Down on the ground again, Edgar stood for a minute or two breathing hard, his eyes cast down on the grass. "I don't know—" he gasped—"I don't know what would have happened to me if you hadn't come."

Joss stared in surprise a moment before he understood that Edgar was trying to show his gratitude, and then he felt sorry for him; he could guess how much it had cost Edgar to say those words. But that did not prevent him from taking his chance.

"I say, Edgar," he said, "can I draw a couple of furrows with that 'aire?" He pointed to the plough and team still standing at the headland.

Edgar looked up suspiciously. "D'you know how to drive that?" he said. The stubble was his to do and he had his reputation as a ploughman to consider.

"Becourse, I do," said Joss, throwing out his chest. "I work on a farm, don't I?"

"All right." Edgar nodded reluctantly—after all, he could hardly refuse—and Joss ran to the plough-handles. He up-ended the share, just as he had watched it done a hundred times, he shouted, "Goo on," to the horses, and they were off.

For the first few yards his wrists swayed a little with the unaccustomed weight; but he had not been three years on a farm for nothing; he knew which way to bear on the handles to keep a furrow straight. Now he could hear the share grating through the soil and roots, he could see the stubble curling up over the breast of his plough as the furrow opened beneath his feet, and it all happened at his command. He felt as if he owned the field and shouted joyfully to the horses, admonishing them by name; he was a ploughman, he was doing man's work, at last. The only trouble was that the horses went too fast and before he knew where he was, he had reached the opposite headland and one furrow was done. He tipped his plough over on its side in proper professional fashion and turned his horses by word of mouth to the beginning of the next furrow.

"Come 'ere, Darky, come 'ere, Flower," he shouted.

Then, having brought his horses right round and set his share for the next furrow, he went back to the one he had just drawn and examined it critically. It was a bit wobbly at the beginning, but the rest of it could compare with any of Edgar's. There should be no wobble, he vowed, about the second; it should run straight from start to finish, straighter than any of Edgar's; it was his last furrow.

"Flow-err! Da-arky!"

He knew just the right throaty remonstrance to summon them to the effort, to appeal to their better nature, as it were, not to fail him; and then, with teeth set and elbows tense, he slid off behind them. Steadying the handles, keeping one eye on the ground and the other on the horses, stumbling along the narrow furrow, all at the same time—it seemed more than one human body was capable of, but somehow he managed it, and the furrow was what he had meant it to be—except where he had hit that elm-root. Suddenly he felt the share drive into the headland and looking up, he saw Edgar coming to meet him, and not only Edgar, but Walter Clary as well. Joss no longer felt as if he owned the field, and the fine ploughman was now just a small boy who ought to have been scaring crows. He hastily brought his team to a stop and began to sidle off to the hedge. But there was no escaping Walter Clary.

"Hey, boy, come you here," he said.

He was a big, tall man with stiff brown side-whiskers, and though in his hearty way he was a kindly man, his whiskers now looked very fierce. Joss trembled as he sidled back and stood before him. He feared the worst and wondered what it would be.

"Do you know what I think?" demanded Walter Clary.

Joss did not answer; that was what he wanted to know himself.

"Well, I'll tell you," said Walter Clary, who fortunately did not expect an answer. "That 'aire furrow you've just drawed is a damn' good 'un, as the saying is. I didn't know you had that in you, boy. Now I'll tell you what I'm going to do."

He clapped a hand on Joss's shoulder and Joss felt his head go round and round.

"Well, I'm going to set you two to work together," Walter Clary went on. "Young Edgar want a mate and that'll keep him up to scratch. So you'll both go to plough on this stubble to-morrow morning. Now then, you young rascals, off to your work, and don't let me catch you up to mischief agin, as the saying is." Anything that Walter Clary said, however trite, was likely, if he chose, to become a "saying."

Joss scuttled back to his field, still hardly daring to think of what was in store for him, in case it might not be true. There was not a rook in the sky, but to show his zeal he lifted up his voice.

"Ee-yar-ico, ee-yar-ico!" It swelled louder and more liquid than ever before. It was a song of triumph.

WALTER CLARY WAS A KNOWING MAN, AND IN RAISING
Joss's status on the farm he had not acted merely from
kind-heartedness. By setting the two boys to work together he created a rivalry between them, which not
only meant that he got more work from each, but also
ensured that his son was more thoroughly grounded in
the several branches of farming practice. Joss, who might
otherwise have been confined to one of them alone, or
even to the less skilled tasks of the general labourer, received the same benefits as Edgar. They learnt the management of horses and all the operations of tillage—
ploughing, harrowing, rolling, horse-hoeing and drilling
—from the chief horseman; they learnt milking, the rearing of calves, the fattening of pigs, from the stockman;
and they were admitted to the minor mysteries of his
craft by the crusty old shepherd. Sometimes one
ploughed the straighter furrow, milked his cows faster,
or built a neater load of hay than the other; but there
was really nothing to choose between them and it was
acknowledged by every one on the farm—except Daddy
Haines, the shepherd, who, for reasons he would not tell,
never had a good word for Edgar. But Daddy Haines

was like that; he was given to arbitrary likes and dislikes, and no one paid much attention to them.

Walter Clary himself had no thought for their mutual feelings; he knew nothing about them. But as it turned out, his plan did much to improve them. In any case neither of the boys was of an age for nursing rancour, and since, whether they liked it or not, they had to put up with each other's company, it was easiest for them to forget, Edgar his grudges and humiliations, Joss his petty triumphs. Being engaged, moreover, in serious rivalry, they came, in the course of their work, to take each other seriously; they began to acquire a respect for each other. They were continually together on the farm, they were used to each other; and so, from mere use and familiarity they gradually passed on to spending their off hours, such as they were, together.

It was natural enough. They were both of the same stock, they had been at school together; they wore the same working clothes and boots, they did the same work, their habits and pleasures were equally the same. The only difference in their lives at this stage was that Edgar ate better and slept softer than Joss; but they had not yet learnt to regard such differences as important. Accordingly they went for long walks together on Sunday afternoons, they looked for birds' nests, they picked bluebells, they gathered blackberries, crabapples and mushrooms, together. They swam in the horsepond together; together they went down to the village of an evening and played quoits, or kicked an old football about on the green, or exchanged gibes with the girls not yet of courting age. Nevertheless, it would not have been right to call them friends. Their relationship was based upon mutual respect, but it was without emotion on either side; nor did it extend to their private lives, for though they were together in the fields, on the roads, or on the village green, neither had ever crossed the other's threshold. It was essentially a relationship of togetherness; as Walter Clary would have put it, they were just "mates."

One March evening, as usual, Joss called for Edgar at the farm to go down and help the blacksmith's boy to mend his football. Joss was now eighteen, he was earning seven shillings a week. He had his hobnailed boots made to measure by the village cobbler, he wore the best corduroy to be had in Brettsleigh; and though still half a head shorter than Edgar, he had grown so square and solid in the chest that he was commonly known on the farm as "the thick 'un." It was lambing-time, and as he and Edgar passed through the stackyard by the lambing-fold, Daddy Haines hailed them.

"Hey, you two," he called, "I want you. Give us a hand here."

Edgar, his mind on the village green and the punctured football, made a grimace. "I reckon our working-day's over, Daddy," he said.

"All right," said the shepherd curtly, "the thick 'un 'll do. Come on, boy, I want you to hold that 'aire ship for me." He pointed to a ewe that was hanging its head and scratching with its hoofs in the loose straw.

Joss knew at once what was wanted. He clambered

over the hurdles and quickly pushed the ewe over on her side, while the shepherd got down on his knees behind her quarters.

"That 'on't be easy," he said, as he passed a hand up between her haunches. "Legs all over the place, I doubt. But I couldn't get to work on her without somebody to hold her down. God's truth!" He broke off and pressing his cheek against the ewe's fleece, buried his forearm in her. For five minutes he remained in this position, apparently motionless, but sweating and grunting with the effort; and then uttered a sigh.

"Good thing I was born with small hands," he said. "That's one leg I've got."

Joss, who was still sitting on the ewe's head and watching him with set face, sighed too. The shepherd resumed his grunting and sweating, and it was five minutes before he sighed again.

"That's the other, you bitch," he gasped. "He's now a-coming."

The exhausted ewe bleated and Joss's face broke into a satisfied smile as he saw, first the shepherd's blood-stained arm appear, relentlessly tugging, and then a head and two forelegs, folded in a trim little parcel. The shepherd changed his grip and the body followed, and after it the clumsy-looking hind legs, all wool and hoofs; it seemed incredible that all that had been inside the ewe. The lamb landed on its side in the straw, but it was on its feet as soon as the shepherd.

"Let her up," he cried to Joss, and seizing the lamb, he dragged it round under its mother's nose, so that she might smell it and know it for her own. He only gave her time for a sniff or two and then began to drag the lamb off towards one of the straw-covered pens at the side of the fold, pausing every yard to make sure she was following the scent. In this way she was lured into the pen and at once settled down to lick her lamb clean. Daddy Haines drew a hurdle in front of her and at last had a chance to wipe the sweat off his face.

"Pore owd dear," he said, gazing compassionately at the ewe, "that wholly wrung her, but I durstn't leave her to fetch help."

Joss put both his elbows on the hurdle and gazed too.

"Nice lamb," he said, "beautiful lamb."

By now Edgar, who had been watching them from the entrance to the fold, was getting impatient.

"Hey, Joss," he said, "ain't you coming?"

The shepherd turned round and Joss pulled himself up off the hurdle. "All right," he said.

"You were suthun slow, together," grumbled Edgar, as Joss walked across to him. "Wasting all that time on an owd ship!"

"Hey, wasting time on an owd ship, eh?" The shepherd came shuffling across through the loose straw. "Now do you listen to me, young Edgar. Do you know what's wrong with you?"

"Half as much as there is with you, I doubt," said Edgar, jeeringly.

"That may be," said the old man, wagging his stick in Edgar's face, "but I'll tell you what that is. Now do you listen here. You'd like to sell a dozen nice fat ship and jingle the money in your pocket, wouldn't you? Yes, but that's all you trouble arter 'em. You don't trouble if they suffer or starve; them ship ain't nothen to you."

"Hark at him a-mobbing me," said Edgar with a sarcastic grin.

"Yes, you may grin," continued the shepherd, "but that's true. We all know you're a good tradesman and can plough a tidy furrow, but you hain't got no heart, not for ship, nit for nothen else, I reckon."

"Oh, come on, Joss, I can't listen to the owd bastard no more," said Edgar, who was beginning to lose his temper. His toes were itching for that football, and what was more, he had an uncomfortable feeling that the old man was right.

"Wait a minute, boy," said the shepherd, as Joss swung his leg out of the fold. "Here's twopence to drink my health down at The Rose. I didn't want to lose that 'aire ewe."

"Why, thank you, Daddy," said Joss in some surprise. A ewe had to be saved whatever happened, and twopence was a great deal out of a shepherd's wages. Still, twopence was twopence and he pocketed it gladly.

"What's that he give you?" said Edgar, as they walked off through the stackyard.

"Twopence to drink his health," said Joss, still fingering the pennies.

"Why, blast," said Edgar, "if I'd ha' knowed that, I'd have went and sat on his owd ewe myself."

"I tell you what," said Joss impulsively. "By then we get to the green, that'll be too dark for football. What about going down to The Rose and having a wet together? I've got twopence more of my own."

Edgar looked black. He had missed his football, the shepherd had made him feel uncomfortable, Joss had earnt twopence and he had not. He no longer cared what he did, but he might as well have his share of the twopence. He shrugged his shoulders.

"Just as you like, bor," he said.

Both of them were already accustomed to beer—it was the regular drink in the fields—but hitherto they had drunk it only to quench their thirst, and not for pleasure. Their pleasures were the adolescent pleasures of growing muscles and the open air, and they had no need of either the social amenities of the public house or the stimulus of alcohol. At odd times Joss had had a drink or two at the back door of The Rose; but since the night when he saw his father taken off to prison, it had never occurred to him to go there in search of an evening's entertainment—and in any case he had had little money to spare for such luxuries. This evening, however, things were different. He had money of his own in his pocket and the shepherd had treated him to the price of a pint as if a pint was his due, as indeed it was. He was a man now and he suddenly felt tempted to try a man's pleasures.

It was still early in the evening when they entered the taproom of The Rose, and nobody from the village had yet arrived. The only other customers were three strangers, seated together in one corner, but they were enough to make Joss and Edgar self-conscious and awkward; it was the public part of the public house that they were not used to. They said good evening and seated themselves rather shrinkingly on a wooden bench in the opposite corner. Then the landlord came in and Joss laid fourpence on the table.

"Quart, please," he said.

"Not many here," said Edgar, while the beer was being drawn.

"No," said Joss, "too soon arter tea."

"Nice evening," said the landlord, as he set their quart on the table.

"Nice evening," said Joss, and pushed the pot along the table to Edgar. "Drink, bor."

"Good health," said Edgar, and took a drink.

"Good health," repeated Joss, and did the same.

For the next ten minutes they sat in silence, taking turn by turn with the quart. The lamps were not yet alight, but there was a good wood fire in the hobbed grate and the framed brewer's advertisements on the walls winked in its soft, mellow glow. The smell of wood-smoke and the dry, beery smell of the taproom itself mingled happily together. They were akin to the smells of barns, stables and stackyards that Joss daily breathed, and he felt at home among them. He felt rested and at ease, and although there was nothing much doing, he wanted nothing more at the moment than to be, and to go on being, in the state in which he found himself. He was glad he had come.

The three strangers sat in their corner and talked quietly among themselves, but one of them, a burly man with a square, sandy beard, stared curiously at Joss, who, on looking at him a second time, seemed to remember his face. At last the man could hold his curiosity no longer.

"I say, boy," he said, bending forward over the table, "are you Matt Elvin's boy—Matt Elvin what went to jail for pulling a swede?"

"Yes, that's right," said Joss, and now he seemed to remember the man's voice as well.

"Ah, I reckoned so," said the man, "but you've wholly altered since then. You see, boy, I was the constable what arrested him."

Joss opened his eyes wide. Of course, he knew the man now, but what was he doing here, what poor man was he after this time? The suspicion in his eyes was so plain that the man laughed out loud at him.

"Don't you worry, my boy," he said. "I ain't a constable no more. I soon jacked up with that job—they reckoned I liked my tea too much." With a wink he held up his mug and swallowed a mouthful.

"Good thing too," he went on, when he had set his mug down. "I was right sick of taking pore bastards up afore the justices for pulling a swede or snaring a rabbit. I drive a dealer's cart now; Kerridge my name, Joe Kerridge—they all know me between Brettsleigh and Ipswich, but I ain't often out this way. But blast, how you've growed, boy! Why, then you warn't nothen but a little owd boy, and now you've got a barrel on you like a bullock. How many years is that since then?"

Joss still felt suspicious of the ex-constable, but he

counted up on his fingers. "That was seven years ago last Michaelmas," he said a bit stiffly.

"Ah, that would be," said Joe Kerridge, nodding, "a year afore I packed up, I remember. Well, you fare better fed than your father did. He looked reg'lar half starved; but blast, what a lovely singer he was! I remember that night I 'rested him I looked in through the winder and heared him a-singing like a lark; and I tell you, I wanted to kick my bloody helmet in the ditch and go straight in and stand him a quart, and arst him to sing another. I can't remember what that was he was a-singing, but that was right a lovely song."

Joss smiled. He seldom thought of Matthew and his songs now, but he could not help warming to a man who praised them both so generously.

"I remember," he said eagerly. "That was *The Young Sailor Cut Down in His Prime.*"

"That's the one," said Joe Kerridge, thumping the table. "That's a lovely song. Now how do that go?"

Joss cocked his eye at the ceiling and hummed the first line:

One day as I strolled along by The Royal Albion—

"Ah, that's right," cried Joe Kerridge. "Go on, my lad."

Joss shook his head and looked sheepish. "I ain't no singer," he mumbled.

"What do that matter?" said Joe Kerridge, turning to his two companions. "We ain't going to find fault with you if you sing a wrong note, are we? I tell you, if you could sing that owd song, that'd wholly please me. Come on, boy."

"Yes, come on," added one of the other two.

Joss licked his lips nervously. "I don't know if I can remember that," he said, and looked up at the ceiling again to gather his faculties. Then he cleared his throat and launched his voice at a venture.

One day as I strolled along by The Royal Albion,
Dark was the morning and bitter the day.
Who should I spy but one of my shipmates,
Wrapped in a blanket far colder than clay?
He called for a candle to light him to bed with,
Also a blanket to wrap round his head.
His poor head was aching, his poor heart was breaking,
For he was a young sailor cut down in his prime.
So we will beat the drums over him and play the fifes
merrily,
Play the dead march as we carry him along.
We will take him to the churchyard and fire three
volleys over him,
For he was a young sailor cut down in his prime.

Joss's throat was still rather hoarse and his voice sounded oddly thin and lonely there in the big room by itself; but line by line the song began to come back to him, and not only the words, but every note of the rather difficult tune—just as his father had sung it, he knew. The chorus came easier and the three men remembered enough to join in, which gave him some confidence. When he started on the second verse, his hoarseness was gone and his voice rang out clear and lusty.

44

His poor aged father, his good old mother,
Often have told him about his past life.
Along with those flash girls his money he squandered,
Along with those flash girls he took his delight.
But now he is dead and laid in his coffin,
Six jolly sailor-boys walk by his side.
Each of them carried a bunch of white roses
So every one might smell them as we passed by.

Just as he was beginning the third verse the taproom
door opened and half a dozen regular customers from
the village tiptoed in and sat down. But Joss was too
thoroughly possessed by his song to mind them now,
and sang on:

At the corner of the street, you will see two girls
    standing.
One to the other did whisper and say,
"Here comes the young sailor whose money we squan-
    dered,
Here comes the young sailor cut down in his prime."
At the top of his tombstone you will see these words
    written:
"Now all you young fellows, take warning of me.
Never go courting the flash girls of the city,
For the flash girls of the city were the ruin of me."
    So we will beat the drums over him and play the
    fifes merrily,
    Play the dead march as we carry him along.
    We will take him to the churchyard and fire three
    volleys over him,
    For he was a young sailor cut down in his prime.

45

By the time he had reached the end of the last chorus, there were a dozen people in the room and Joss was quite taken aback by their combined applause. One of them, a squat man with a wooden leg, in a square-tailed brown velvet coat and red-speckled corduroy trousers, stumped across and clapped him on the shoulder. It was Tod Jordan, the hurdle-maker.

"Ah, we've got a singer at The Rose agin," he said. "Fill up his quart pot, landlord."

"No, no, I'm standing that," protested Joe Kerridge, "I arst him to sing."

"That's all right," said Tod Jordan. "You can pay for the next, bor. He's his father's son. He'll drink that."

Joss grinned with delight. It was not merely that he was in the limelight, although he could not help liking that. But the whole scene—the flickering grate, the buzz of voices, the beer, the company, the good song— it was all as he had watched it through the window in his father's time, only now he was on the right side of the window. If these were a man's pleasures, he liked them, and he had never been so glad to be his father's son.

"Here you are, my boy," said the landlord, bringing in another quart. "Drink and drink hearty. That's lovely beer. That's paid for."

For the first time since he had started to sing Joss turned to Edgar. In all the excitement he had quite forgotten Edgar's presence, but now he wanted him to share his own pleasure.

"Drink, bor," he said.

46

But Edgar shook his head. All through Joss's song and the subsequent applause he had sat there feeling he ought to be a better man than Joss; but something in his head kept telling him that he was not, that, after all that had happened that night, Joss was the better man. He felt he had a grievance and though he wanted to share the pleasure, he could not. Indeed, he could bear it no longer.

"I've had enow, Joss," he said. "I must now be a-going. I hain't fed my ferrets."

"He's a funny young feller, ain't he?" said Joe Kerridge, as Edgar, somewhat red in the face, pulled himself up from his seat and walked to the door.

"Oh, he's all right," said Joss stoutly. "He's my mate, he is." He tipped up the quart pot.

TOD JORDAN CAME OF A SETTLED LABOURING FAMILY, but he had early married a "travelling" half-bred gypsy and taken to the road with her. Then one day their horse had run away on a steep hill and Tod, after barely a year of married life, had lost both his wife and his own right leg; but although he had given up the road after that, he still lived in his caravan and was still regarded by his neighbours as half a "traveller." He was commonly known as a hurdle-maker and was reputed to be able to put a hurdle together in less than half an hour, but that was only a small part of his trade, for Tod was also a skilled woodman. All the winter and most of the autumn he was busy in woods and coverts, cutting out the small timber he had bought and carting innumerable loads of poles and faggots, which he spent the rest of the year in disposing of. The faggots he generally sold as he had cut them, for kindling or peasticks; but the poles became anything he could fashion from them —stakes, clothes-props, linen-posts or walking-sticks—and he had a special line in wooden rakes, which he hawked about all over the countryside in haysel and harvest.

The trade in these days was still good and Tod made a steady living. He had been able to buy a little meadow in a distant part of the parish, where he kept his caravan and had built a rough shed to house the great copper in which he boiled crooked poles straight and straight poles crooked, his sawing-horse, his hand-lathe, hooks, bills, axes, saws and other tools, his two old dogcarts and his roan cob. He could afford all the food and clothes he wanted and all the beer he could drink, which was a good deal; he could take a day off when he chose. He preferred now to live alone, but he was by no means a solitary. In his brown velvet square-tailed coat, or "frock," and his "pheasant" cord trousers, he was known and welcomed at all the public houses for miles around, and despite his wooden leg, he was still, in his early middle life, well seen by the women. Tod had no desire to change his lot.

The time came when Walter Clary could no longer do without a new trap to uphold his prestige in Brettsleigh market, and not being very flush, he bethought himself of Ditch Wood. Ditch Wood was an outlying copse of ten acres that belonged to the farm; the brushwood, or "slop," had not been cut out of it for twenty years and ought to be worth something, he reckoned. He turned it over in his mind for a week or two, until one day the shepherd asked him for some more hurdle-poles.

"You shall have 'em," he said. "Do you wait till we cut Ditch Wood."

The next thing he did was to go and see Tod, who a few hours earlier had been informed of his intention by Daddy Haines and had already laid his plans.

"I want the slop cut out of Ditch Wood," said Walter Clary. "How much'll you bid me for that?"

"H'm," said Tod, pretending to look surprised, "that's a tidy big wood, Mr. Clary, and that hain't been done for a long time."

"Yes, and that'll be worth all the more," said Walter Clary.

" 'Haps that will, 'haps that 'on't," said Tod, still rather backward-seeming, "but that'll take me all the winter."

"Still, there's lovely stuff there, bor," said Walter Clary coaxingly. "Ash poles as big as your thigh, hazel thick as your arm. Come on, Tod, what'll you bid me?"

Tod pursed his lips. He had had his eye on Ditch Wood for years, he knew there was good stuff there; but he was in no hurry.

"I tell you what I'll do, Mr. Clary," he said after a long pause. "I'll give you a pound an acre for that, but you'll have to lend me a man to help me cut that. Yes, I'll pay his wages," he added, as Walter Clary raised his eyebrows.

Walter Clary looked at his boots and nodded. "I don't know who I could spare," he said.

"I want Joss Elvin," declared Tod, so that there might be no doubt about it.

"Well, you can't have him," said Walter Clary bluntly. "I can't spare him."

"Well, you can keep your slop," said Tod, no less bluntly. "I hain't only got one leg and I can't manage all that heavy stuff by myself."

"But Joss is one of the best men I've got," protested Walter Clary.

"That's just why I want him," said Tod. "Them thick 'uns are the right sort for wood-cutting work. 'Sides, he's a comfortable owd boy. I like him."

Walter Clary looked at his boots again, but what he saw was the black and yellow dogcart that Martin Wright used to drive in to Brettsleigh. It was the exact cart he wanted himself.

"Well, 'haps I could let you have him for a week or two," he said.

"That'll be till the job's done, or nothen," said Tod. "But you'll have him back in time for haysel, I doubt."

Walter Clary went on looking at his boots and frowned, but he could not wait any longer for his trap.

"Can we settle first then?" he said, looking up sharply.

"When you like, Mr. Clary," said Tod with the blandest of smiles; but although the ten gold sovereigns were in his pocket ready counted out, he did not intend to part with them here in the fields. "I shall be down at The Rose to-night," he said.

Walter Clary frowned again. He knew that would cost him a quart; but at least he would have his trap by next market-day.

"All right," he said, turning on his heel, "you can have Joss in a fortnit."

Much as he disliked it, Walter Clary kept his word, and early one morning in December Joss set out to meet Tod at Ditch Wood. Joss himself was looking forward to this change from the ordinary round of farm work, and none the less, he discovered, because it also meant a change from Edgar.

He and Edgar were still mates; they still worked together and went about together. But since the previous spring and their first evening together at The Rose, something seemed to have happened to Edgar. He was reserved and silent, even to the point of coolness, and though he still went to The Rose with Joss, he would never stop if Joss was called upon to sing, which now he frequently was. Joss, who viewed things simply, as he saw them, could make nothing of him. He did not know, and it did not occur to him to suspect, that Edgar now regarded him as the better man of the two and bore him a grudge for it, a grudge that revived all the old grudges, for years half forgotten, as far back as their schooldays; he did not know that Edgar's mind was again set on somehow getting his own back and showing himself, by hook or crook, the better man. But that was how things stood; and naturally he could not comprehend why Edgar continually behaved as if he was tired of his company and yet did nothing to avoid it. The one thing that was clear to Joss was that most of the time Edgar's company made him feel uneasy, and he was glad at the prospect of having less of it. After all, you could be mates, and perhaps even better mates, without working together.

With Tod Jordan it was just the opposite. Joss had seen a good deal of him at The Rose during the past few months and it was generally Tod who called upon him to sing. With his encouragement, Joss was gradually mastering all his father's songs and learning to pick up new ones as he heard them, and in some measure, he had already begun to take his father's old place at The Rose. Tod had stood him many a quart and in Tod's company he was always at his ease. If Tod was the same in the woods as he was at The Rose, he looked forward to his new master.

Ditch Wood was separated from the road by a strip of derelict land in notable contrast to Walter Clary's well-tilled fields. Nothing had been done to stop it from going down to bushes, and there was now very little grass to be seen between the thorns, briars and brambles that covered it and sheltered its swarming rabbits. From the road this wilderness was suitably ushered in by a small cottage and buildings, also derelict, and well on the way to ruin. This was, in fact, old Chaffinch's cottage, the decline of which, in the past, Joss himself had assisted; but the old man had been dead some years and it was now uninhabited. It was still known as Chaffinch's, however, and as it was a convenient landmark, Tod Jordan had made it their rendezvous.

When Joss arrived at half past seven with his hook under his arm, Tod had already stowed his horse and trap in the yard and was standing by the gate, smoking. With his little, twinkling eyes, deep in a network of wrinkles, his big, loose mouth, his high cheekbones and grizzled, mutton-chop whiskers, he looked as if he was having a perpetual joke with himself. He was still well built and remarkably active, in spite of his wooden leg.

"You 'on't need that till arter breakfast," he said, pointing to the hook under Joss's arm. "We'll go and have a look round first."

Joss dropped the hook under Tod's trap and they plodded silently up to the edge of the wood with Tod's snaky black lurcher at their heels. It was a cold, misty morning and neither was in the mind for conversation. When they reached the edge of the wood, Tod paused and looked along a wide drift that led off among the trees.

"Yes, Walter Clary was right," he said. "There's wholly some stuff there. Do you look, boy. Ash poles, hazel poles, maple poles—I like a bit of maple, that don't rot where that go into the ground—and everlasting o' faggots. There's some hard work for you there, Joss."

Tod contemplated his timber for a minute or two more, but he made no attempt to examine it more closely.

"Let's have a look this way," he said, and turned up along the ditch that skirted the wood. "I doubt there's an owd rabbit lay there," he said, as the lurcher jumped into the ditch and began nosing among the bushes. "Yes, bor, blast—he's off."

They could no longer see the lurcher, but they could hear his excited scamperings among the dead leaves; and suddenly a rabbit broke cover. It raced off along a newly ploughed water furrow and a second later the lurcher flung himself after it. At first the rabbit drew away and the lurcher looked like an ungainly black ball bouncing behind it. Then he flattened out into a gallop and the bouncing black ball became a black streak sliding in the furrow, and sliding ever nearer to the rabbit's tail. At last, when there was scarcely a couple of yards between them, the rabbit swerved sideways out of the furrow. At the same moment the lurcher put on a spurt that brought his jaws to the rabbit's neck. The jaws snapped.

"Oh, well done, Dash!" cried Tod, as the lurcher turned round with the rabbit in his mouth and began to lope back along the furrow.

"As pretty a sight as ever I seed," said Joss. "He's right a courser, he is."

"Good owd dog, good owd dog," said Tod, as he took the rabbit from the lurcher's mouth and felt its back. "And a lovely rabbit, fat as a mole, Joss."

He cut a slit in the fur of one of its hind legs and forcing the other leg through it till the hocks were crossed, he made himself a loop to carry it by. Then, with the rabbit swinging on a crook'd finger and the lurcher behind him, sniffing it affectionately, he stumped on along the ditch.

"Several rabbits along here," he said. "See where they've been a-gnoring that ash-stub. A rabbit wholly like an owd ash-stub winter-time. Blast, boy, look at that 'aire."

There was a wide ring of rabbit-holes at the foot of a small pollard elm and Dash was now busy thrusting his nose into each of them. When he had finished, he sat down in the bottom of the ditch with his nose pointing at the burrow.

"Look, he've owned that," said Tod, "and look at the

55

tracks and all that fresh earth. I reckon that owd root is a-jumping with rabbits. We must have them out of there. What do you say, boy?"

Joss nodded and grinned. Rabbiting was sport to him; it was a good deal better than work.

"Walter Clary 'on't mind a rabbit or two," continued Tod, "and I've got my ferrets and nets down in the trap —lucky I brought 'em, ain't that?—so we'll now go and have breakfast afore we start."

"Couldn't we have that here?" said Joss, who was beginning to feel hungry and had got his food in a small sack slung over his shoulder. "We could easy find a dry perk in the wood."

"Here?" said Tod scornfully. "What's the sense in having breakfast here, when we've got a roof to our hids and a hearth to set by?"

"What, Chaffinch's, you mean?" said Joss, but hardly believing it.

"What else?" said Tod. "Why, afore you came, bor, I'd got a fire in the grate and the kettle on. I like a cup of hot tea to my breakfast, don't you?"

For answer Joss grinned again; he, too, liked a cup of hot tea on a morning like this, but he seldom got it.

"Well, there's a rum 'un for you," said Tod, as they descended to the cottage, "to see smoke a-coming out of that 'aire."

The one tottery chimneypot vigorously belching above a patch of naked rafters was an odd enough sight by itself, but to make it odder still, the once orderly inmates of the garden had joined hands with wild in-

56

truders to make the rest of the house invisible. Plum and apple branches thick with barren suckers, rank laurels and a giant box hedge jostled with elders and sycamores above the eaves; hops, ivy and wild clematis piled themselves in heaps on what was left of the thatch and hung in festoons from the gables. With the chimney smoking in the middle, it all looked like a vast bonfire ready to burst into flame. Joss and Tod had to fight their way to the doorstep.

"There," said Tod, pausing on the threshold to rest, "we shall have to get to work with the hook if we're going to set up house here. And to think that this was one of the neatest, prettiest little gardens you ever did see; that wholly used to grow some stuff, I tell you. And the cottage, too, plumb in the middle. There warn't a cleaner, dryer house in Overham, and look at that now. Plaster a-coming off in lumps, laths a-sticking out, not a pane of glass in the winders—and that was you little bastards from the village as started that. You broke his winders, you pulled his thatch down, you dragged the door off its hinjles."

He glared at Joss, who, for the first time face to face with the whole desolation of Chaffinch's and unable to deny his own small share in it, felt ashamed. To avoid Tod's accusing glare he pushed through the doorway and began to explore.

The doorway gave into a little transverse passage, which provided access, immediately in front, to the winding staircase, and, at either end, to the two ground-floor rooms. The room in which he first found himself had obviously been the kitchen. It was a little, narrow room with one window and was fitted with a little hobbed grate and a Dutch oven at the side of it. The stove was rusty and the oven, torn from its cavity in the wall, was lying on the floor; but both were still in better condition, Joss noted, than the stove and the oven in his mother's cottage. The walls had shed a good deal of plaster, but there was nothing wrong with the solid-beamed and whitewashed ceiling or the wooden shelves of the big storeroom, which ran the whole length of one side of the kitchen; they would hold a fine lot of food, Joss thought.

From the back of the kitchen a door opened into the backhouse, a one-storey lean-to with a tiled roof. There were chinks between the tiles, through which strands of ivy had crept, to hang, pale, etiolated streamers, in the half-darkness; but they had done no harm to the massive copper or the still more massive bush-oven, for which the backhouse had once largely existed. The bush-oven, in particular, was built out from the main kitchen chimney-breast and stood shoulder-high on stout brick piers. Its wide mouth was curved and hooded like a small well-head, and there was room inside for the whole of a very big faggot. Joss stood and stared at it in wonder. He had never seen a batch of bread as big as that oven would bake; it made him hungry to look at it.

Hunger soon put an end to his staring, and calling to mind the cup of tea Tod had promised him, he strolled round through the kitchen to the parlour, on the other side of the house. It was a bigger room than the kitchen, but the floor was so littered with all sorts of rubbish that there was not much space left to move. There was a huge square bedstead made of old tarred railings and unbarked poles, roughly nailed together, a chair and a table knocked together out of packing-cases and bristling with jagged nails, an old flock mattress discharging its contents from all four corners, a pair of old boots and several articles of ragged clothing. There was also a heap of soot overflowing the hearth, but in spite of that Tod had got a good fire going in the little bow-fronted grate and was in the act of filling a brown china teapot from the kettle. Two enamel mugs with milk, sugar and teaspoons in them stood ready at his feet.

"That fare good," said Joss, squatting down on the edge of the bedstead and starting to undo the handkerchief his food was wrapped in.

"Yes, bor," said Tod, putting the kettle back on the fire, "I believe in making myself comfortable."

Joss took a hunk of bread and a bit of cold bacon in one hand, shaved off a morsel of each with his shut-knife, and put them in his mouth.

"You know, Tod," he said with his mouth still half full, "the owd house ain't right what you'd call done for. The ceilings and floors, the inside walls—there ain't much amiss with 'em; and that master gret bush-oven!"

"I know," said Tod. "That only want toiting up a bit." He filled the two mugs from the teapot and handed one to Joss. "That's nice and strong, boy," he said, "and plenty of milk and sugar."

"Well, what I can't make out," said Joss, stirring hard

at his mug, "what I can't make out is why somebody don't take and toit that up."

"Well, bor," said Tod, and paused to swallow a large lump of cold pig's trotter. "Well, you see, that ain't so easy as that fare. You don't know nothen of the legal business, I doubt?"

"No," said Joss, "I know owd Chaffinch was crazed, pòre owd devil, that's all."

"Well, I'll tell you what that is," said Tod. "Owd Chaffinch was a saddler in Brettsleigh and that fare he'd allus wanted to have a cut at farming. Then one day an owd uncle left him this place—round twenty acres, that was—and being as he'd saved a bit, he gave up his business and came out here. Well, the truth was, he warn't used to farming, and when he set to work on these here fields—mind you, they warn't in a bad way when he took 'em—anyhow they soon got the master of him and ran away with all his money; and then, on top of that, his wife took cold and died—she allus did complain of the draughts—and the pore owd man got sillier and sillier, till he went right off his hid."

"Yes," said Joss, "but why didn't they put him out of the way and have a steward, or sell the farm?"

"Ah, yes, but that warn't so simple," said Tod. "You see, I said the owd uncle left him the farm, but that warn't altogether his'n. That was left to him for his life, but arter his death that was to go to owd Chaffinch's niece. Well, while owd Chaffinch was alive they couldn't take that away from him 'cause that belonged to this here gal as well, and when he died, she'd gone to Australia and they couldn't find her. That was ten year ago and they still haint found her."

"But why couldn't they sell that and keep the money for when they find her?" said Joss with a shocked look. "Letting good land go to waste like that! That ain't right."

Tod shrugged his shoulders. "That's the law, bor," he said, "and the law ain't for the likes of us to make out. Still, I have heared that might be sold one day, and I'll tell you for why. The owd man, arter he got crazed, never paid no rates and he cost the Guardians a shilling or two a week in pore relief, and when he died, they gave him a pauper funeral. Well, now that fare they want to get their money back, and a bloke what know the clurk told me he reckon anybody could have that as'd give 'em what's owing. That'd make fifty quid look silly, he say."

"I'm glad to hear that," said Joss.

"'Haps you are," continued Tod sarcastically, "but what's the good of that now? Who's going to give two quid and more an acre and pull up all them owd briars and bushes, and then pare and burn, and pick out all the speargrass and bines? Why, that'd drive you as crazed as owd Chaffinch."

Joss thoughtfully cut himself another sliver of bacon. "All the same, that ain't right," he said, "not when pore folks are starving."

Tod laughed. "Well, you ain't starving, bor," he said. "Drink up your tea and don't you fret."

Joss laughed too and drank his mugful. "That's wholly

a nice cup of tea," he said, smacking his lips and looking round him with satisfaction, as the warmth of it spread over his stomach. "You know, Tod, I like that here. I reckon we'll toit that up a bit afore we've done."

" 'Haps we will," said Tod, "but we'd better see arter them rabbits first, I doubt."

Half an hour later they were both on their knees in the ditch at the edge of the wood. All the holes in the burrow but one were stopped with handfuls of grass or netted with coarse string nets. Tod was putting a ferret on a long line down the one free hole, Joss was watching the nets. The lurcher sat in the grass and looked on benignly; he had told them there were rabbits in the burrow and now, unless any escaped, his work was done.

"He's a-going, he's a-going," said Tod, paying out line. "Ah, now, he've stopped." He put his ear to the hole and listened. "I can hear 'em a-scrabbing, bor. Ah, here he is, back agin. He's blooded, bor. Keep your eye on them nets."

Joss stepped from one side of the burrow to the other and made a grab, as a grey-brown ball appeared in the slack of one of the nets. He slipped a hand under and pulled it out, seized it by the head and hind legs, gave the head a twist, and tossed it in the withered grass. The lurcher got up and nosed it, and snapped as it gave a few last, convulsive kicks.

"Look out, bor, he's a-travelling," said Tod, now up to his elbow in the hole.

Joss stepped across the burrow again and grabbed another rabbit, which he treated in the same manner.

"There's plenty more where they come from," said Tod. "He's still a-travelling."

Joss knelt down again to watch the nets and at that moment the mid-morning sun came out, glinting on the bare blackthorn stems and softening the pallor of the withered grass. Joss, still warm inside from his breakfast, received its warmth on his cheek and felt suddenly glad, glad he was there and nowhere else, and doing the thing he was doing. He had no animosity against the rabbits —though the mischief they did might have merited it— and he took no pleasure in killing them; but he liked rabbiting. He liked kneeling there in the withered grass with his hands in the fresh-burrowed subsoil and his head against an ash-stub, he liked watching the nets for the grey-brown ball to appear and being warmed by the sunshine. He had no idea why he liked these things; but they made him feel happy, not so much in the more wide-awake human way as passively and half unconsciously, like a wild creature at one with its surroundings. But though he was happy, he was earning his living and helping to earn Tod's. At the end of half an hour six stiff, furry corpses were lying on the ground beside him.

"There's one more," said Tod, tugging at the line, "but I don't know where that is. Why, blast, I do believe he's going up that owd elem. Quick, Joss, that's holler, I reckon."

Joss scrambled up the pollard elm and was just in time to grab a rabbit emerging from a big ivy cluster. "Got you, John," he said triumphantly, as he slid down. "Got you, John."

Tod had retrieved his ferret from the elm-trunk and was clumsily scratching its little, creamy-white head. "Pore owd boy, pore owd boy, then," he said. "You've done a good morning's work."

Then, while Joss cut a pole to sling the rabbits on, he started gutting them and "hurdling" up their hind legs ready for slinging.

"Lovely rabbits," he said, turning out the belly-fat for Joss to see. "You must take a brace home, boy."

"Hullo," said Joss, as he dragged his pole out of the hedge, "who's that a-coming up from Chaffinch's?"

Tod looked round and then with a grin went on with his gutting. "I know who that is," he said. "That's Iky Wolff, what go round a-buying up owd hins for the Whitechapel Jewboys."

"What do he want here?" said Joss.

"Well," replied Tod, "I did a bit of business with him last week at Brettsleigh, and he said he'd try and get me an order. I told him I should be up here, but blast, I never thowt he'd find the way. He's a good owd boy; like his beer all right too."

Iky Wolff was curly-whiskered, bespectacled and Jewish-looking; and in his bowler hat, his shabby black clothes and dirty white collar, he was a strange sight for Ditch Wood.

"A nice dance you've led me 'ere," he gasped in unfamiliar cockney, as he stumbled up to them. "If I'd 'ave known what it was like, you could 'ave gone up to the smoke yourself. But I just can't 'elp being kind, can I? Look at my feet!" He pointed down at his clay-plastered boots and beamed all over his face.

Tod laughed. "Well, what's the news, Iky?" he said.

"All right, my boy," said Iky, tapping him confidentially on the chest. "They want two thousand broomsticks, 'andles, poles—I dunno what you call 'em—afore the New Year. It's a big toolshop in Bow—near where I live. I know the manager." He tapped Tod again and winked. "Give you a good price—what I told you; you can pay me my commission when you get your money. Is it on?"

"That'll do, bor," said Tod with a wide, satisfied grin. "They can have forty thousand if they like. I'll stand treat, Iky, next time I see you in Brettsleigh."

"That's just what I thought you'd do, Tod," said Iky, "but I knew I should get thirsty afore then." With another wink he pulled two pint bottles from an inside pocket. "One for me and one for you," he said, handing one to Tod.

"That's famous," said Tod. "I wholly like a wet when I'm out rabbiting—and I never know where to get one. There ain't no public housen in these here coverts. Well, here's your health, Iky."

He put the bottle to his mouth and tipped it up.

"That was beautiful," he said, wiping his mouth on

the back of his hand. "Come on, Joss. We'll share this between us."

"I didn't know how much I wanted that till I had that," said Joss, when he had taken a pull.

"I say, Tod," said Iky, pointing to the seven rabbits laid out stiff on the grass, "I thought you were supposed to be cutting poles."

Tod burst out laughing. "Quite right," he said, "but I tell you, Iky, that's like this here. I work for my living and I want enow to live on, and live on well. But why should I go on a-slaving every minute so's to make more'n I want? Why shouldn't I enjoy myself and have a bit of sport when I've got the chance? That's what I say."

"I don't blame you," said the Jew, tapping his bottle. "I like to enjoy myself too."

"Becourse," Tod went on, "I shall allus be pore, I doubt, but pore folks can enjoy theirselves. What's that song about the pore owd couple?—'What a pore couple were they!' Do you know that one, Joss?"

"Yes," said Joss, "I heared that the other day at Little Gazing Hoss-shoes."

"Come on, out with that, boy," said Tod. "He's a rare singer, Ike, he is."

With a drop of good beer in him, Joss was ready to enjoy himself too. "I'll try what I can do," he said, and without any more preliminaries he started up.

There was an owd couple and they were pore,
Lived in a house with only one door.
What a rum couple were they!

The good owd man, he went out one day
And left his owd woman at home to stay.
  Oh, what a bad woman was she!
The clurk of the parish passed that way.
She called him in by the wink of her eye.
  Oh, what a bad woman was she!
The good owd man, he came home at last.
Tried the door and found it fast.
  Oh, what a rum couple were they!
"Oh, where have you been since I've been gone?"
Artful, artful, diderol day.
"I've been sick since you've been gone.
If you'd been in the garden, you'd have heard me moan."
  Oh, what a rum couple were they!
"One favour I'll ask you to do for me.
Go and fetch me an apple from yonder tree."
"Oh, that will I do," cried he.
As he was climbing up this tree,
She let the clurk out and away run he.
  "That's cleverly done," cried she.

  " ' "That's cleverly done," cried she,' " bellowed Tod.
"That please me, that song do. Here, do you finish the
bottle, Joss."

  "I say," said the Jew, who all through the song had
been looking Joss up and down, "is our young friend
'ere a bruiser or a weight-lifter, or one of these 'ere
blokes as 'ave paving-stones broke on their chests?"

  "No, bor," said Tod, "he's just a labouring man like
me. What made you think that?"

  "Well, 'e's got such a 'ell of a chest on 'im," said
Iky. " 'E's a thick 'un, 'e is."

67

"That's just what we say," said Tod. "We call him 'the thick 'un.' "

"I tell you what," said Iky, "I know just the job for 'im. There's an 'ouse I use up Bow way—know the landlord well, and 'is customers are pretty rough stuff. You know, a fight in the back yard every night and a dozen on Sunday. Well, I know 'e's been looking for just such a lad as 'im for potman—though that 'ain't so much for potman as chucker-out. 'Ow'd you like that, my boy?"

"Yes, how'd you like that, boy?" said Tod, himself curious to hear what Joss would say.

"What, d'you mean me?" said Joss. "Me work in a public up at London?"

"That's it, cully," said Iky. "I could easy speak to the landlord."

Joss looked at him and blinked. London itself meant nothing to him; but he knew what leaving Tod meant, leaving the new master who gave him hot tea for breakfast and then, instead of setting him to work, took him out rabbiting, who called for a song in the middle of the morning. He was not such a fool, even if the Jew thought he was.

"Thank you kindly," he said, laughing sheepishly and shaking his head. "I'm half tidy, where I am."

"All right, I only arst," said Iky. "But if ever you want a change, you just go to The Inkerman near Bow Bridge and arst for Alf Summers. 'E'll only want one look at you, I reckon. Well, Mr. Jordan, if I ain't got my potman, I've got my poles, and now I must be off

68

to Brettsleigh to pick up some fowls. See you next market-day, cully. You can keep the bottles."

"He's a lad," said Tod, as he watched him stumble off across the clods. "And now, Joss, boy, if you'd go and get the hooks, I reckon we might do a stroke of work."

JOSS TOOK UP AN ELM-SWITCH AND HOLDING IT FIRM
under his foot, he kept on twisting with his hands till
it was as pliant as an osier and the thin end could be
bent over and twisted into a loop. Then he laid the
switch on the ground and heaped a bundle of hazel-
boughs on it bigger than himself; he slipped the butt
end of his switch through the loop and setting his foot
on the loop, pulled the bind up tight till the boughs
inside it creaked. He doubled the butt end back and
wound its twisted fibres round themselves—here was the
whole art of the tie—so that they made a sort of crude
rosette, which would prevent the bind from ever slipping. All that remained was to tuck the butt end in
among the boughs, and another faggot was done. The
hazel-boughs would dry out and shrink, but the elm
bind would shrink with them and grip them always
tighter. Joss picked it up with one hand as if it had been
a sheaf of corn, and carried it over to the pile at the
side of the drift, handy for carting. There was not much
about tying a faggot that Joss did not know. He had
been tying faggots all the winter and this was but one
among hundreds.

The faggot in place, he spread his arms out against

the pile for a rest and gazed down the drift. It was nearly the end of March. The first wood anemones, the last sweet violets, and primroses in spring luxuriance, lurked among the nut-stubs; a few hawthorn buds were bursting and an elm sapling had gone purple with bloom; but what Joss gazed at was the sun. It was now well on its downward course and shone straight along the drift into the enormous clearing he had made. It was not actually very warm, but it made the whole wood look warm. The oak-trunks shone silver, the hazel-boughs glowed like brown velvet, and even the tufts of half-dead grass in the drift were nuggets of pure gold. A man who works out of doors in winter-time may well be sensitive to the weather. There is nothing between him and the frost, the wind and the rain that are too often his background, and gentler skies are a respite to be marked and enjoyed. So Joss gazed at the sun and was grateful for it. The wood was very quiet and still, and he was the only human creature in it. He understood now what it was that had made Tod Jordan say over and over again: "I'm never so happy as when I'm in an owd wood."

In the wood it was always warmer than out in the fields and there was always shelter from wind and rain; there was always a stump to sit on or a tree to lean against while you ate your dinner. The work itself was clean and straightforward, and although it consisted mainly of cutting and tying, there was always something new to see—a badger's earth, a prowling fox, a giant toadstool—and with Tod, there was always something new to learn about wood. The right ash sapling for a walnut-brushing pole, the right hazel-boughs for riving into a thatcher's broaches or for making clothes-pegs, an elm post to go under water, a maple to drive in the ground, a piece of "nave," or wych, elm for a beetle hammer, how to choose them and where to find them—these things were but a drop in the well of Tod's vast knowledge. He knew every wood and covert for twenty miles around and could tell you all their timber, sometimes down to a single hornbeam or poplar.

But Tod was not always busy with wood. He would spend a whole morning, if he felt inclined, digging out rabbits or coursing hares with his lurcher; and if as sometimes happened, one of his friends brought a full jar or bottle along, all work was stopped till it was empty. Joss shared these diversions as a matter of course, and they did not prevent him from working just as hard for Tod as he had ever worked for Walter Clary. But they gave him a feeling of independence such as he had not tasted before. He worked when he liked and played when he liked, it seemed, and at times when Tod was away on other business and left him to himself for days on end, it was almost as if he was his own master.

From the beginning, in the same way as Tod, Joss had taken naturally to this life in the woods, but now he had a special reason of his own for doing so. Two months ago his mother had caught a cough and, with little to live for and little will left to live, she had faded, with pious resignation, into the grave.

"Don't be sorry for me, Joss," she had said. "My eyes already behold the golden floor. But you'll wholly miss me, I fear."

Joss had dutifully mourned and buried her, but now that she was dead, he did not miss her as she had prophesied. On the contrary, he felt free, as he had never been before, and to make himself freer still—for unlike Tod, he had no taste for solitary housekeeping—he had sold his few poor sticks and taken lodgings in the village. They were decent working men's lodgings and in some respects more comfortable than his own home had ever been; but nevertheless, he very soon discovered that their comfort could not be compared with the comfort, however meagre, of his own home, his own private place, where he could do as he liked. That was what he missed now, and that was what the wood in some measure restored to him. There he could do as he liked and there was no one to watch him; it almost was his own place. . . .

As Joss leant against the faggot-pile, enjoying the sunshine on his face and the stillness of the wood, there was a sharp crack in the distance, but he took no notice of it; an oak-tree often shed a dead branch with a crack like that. This crack, however, was followed by another and another, and then by a steady swishing noise, as of some one forcing his way through the undergrowth. The wood was evidently not so private as he had imagined, but who could it be? Tod was away for the day at Brettsleigh market. Edgar, he remembered, was cutting a hedge two or three fields away from the wood, but Edgar knew the paths and would not come crashing through the slop like that. Besides, ever since they had ceased working together, Edgar had been going about with a farmer's son from Brettsleigh way, and had deliberately kept his distance. There was no doubt now that Edgar had had enough of him, and once the thing was over, Joss was not sorry. He had a new mate now, and a better one, in Tod, and there was the wood —he could never have shared that with Edgar. Still, though it could not be Edgar, it must be somebody, for the swishing and crackling still went on in the distance, and Joss, feeling that anything whatever that went on in the wood was his business, sauntered down the drift to have a look.

This part of the wood was still uncleared and about a hundred yards along the drift a path led off among the bushes. It was so tangled up with brambles and crisscrossed hazel-boughs as to be scarcely recognizable as a path, but since the noise seemed to come from that direction, Joss stood still in the drift there and waited. He was right. The noise came nearer and nearer, and after two or three minutes a pair of dark-blue sleeves appeared among the bushes, followed, a second later, by a floppy straw hat with a big bow of black ribbon in front of it. Joss stared very hard at these things and then, dragging her skirts by main force from the brambles, a young woman staggered out into the drift. She was dressed in a capacious skirt of brown wincey and a short but full-hipped jacket of dark-blue cloth; the jacket was undone in front and revealed the innumerable

74

buttons of a tight-fitting bodice then known to fashion as a Garibaldi, together with a narrow white tucker at the neck. She looked neat, but the primness of her clothes bespoke the working girl, and Joss felt quite at his ease with her. It was a good thing he did, because as soon as she caught sight of him, she ran up and seized him by the arm.

"Oh, dear, oh, dear," she gasped, "I'm that glad to see some one."

The jet buttons on her bodice went up and down with every breath, her cheeks were flushed, and there were tears on the lashes of her dark eyes. It all suited her very well and Joss smiled approvingly.

"What's the matter, miss?" he said.

"I'm lost," she said, shaking her head in despair. "They told me to take the drift across the wood and I should be in the village in no time. I couldn't miss that, they said."

"Who's 'they'?" said Joss inquisitively.

"Up at the farm, Foxburrows," she said. "I'm the new maid, you see, and Mr. Clary have just started to have the newspaper. That's left at the post office every day and Missis told me I must run across and fetch that in time for tea. 'That'll be one of your duties,' she say. Well, she shew me the path to the wood and told me to take the drift, so I took the drift. But that twisted and turned all ways, and then got all owd nettles and bushes, so's I could hardly walk. And I'd forgot the way back, so I had to go on, and the mud was up to my ankles."

75

She drew back her long skirt to display the toes of her heavy lace-boots.

"Well, that warn't right," said Joss with some warmth, "that warn't right to send you out by yourself. You can easy get lost in a wood like this. Why, I tell you, I've heared of some one as did. That was a telegraph boy from Brettsleigh and he was bringing one of these here telegrams to Foxburrows. Well, they told him in the village to go across Ditch Wood and he did; and he got off the drift and he strayed about in them bushes for three hours, for three hours he did. Then that got dark and he was so frit he started to holler. Well, that happened owd Alfred Eadie—he used to live in a cottage up by the farm—he'd been up to The Rose for a pint, and on his way back he heared the boy a-hollering, so he went into the wood and found him, and took him on to the farm. Do, the boy might be hollering there still."

"Oh, dear, oh, dear," said the girl, clasping her hands and looking scared, "what a dreadful place!"

"Oh, don't you be frit, miss," said Joss hastily. "I'll take you right to the end of the drift and show you the way into the village so's you really can't miss that."

"That's wholly kind of you," she said with a shy smile, and stepped on briskly along the drift beside him.

After a few steps Joss turned his head for a covert glance at her. She was of middle height and well set up, not too plump and not too thin, just right, in fact. Her face, but for a small, pointed chin, was oval and her delicate nose, a true Grecian, continued the line of her high white forehead. She had pink cheeks, large brown eyes and thick, well-shaped lips. Conscious of his eyes on her, she, too, turned her head and looked at him inquiringly.

"You don't come from about here?" said Joss, caught in the act and making the best of it. A girl as striking as she was, a girl with a nose like that, was not likely to escape his notice ten miles away.

"No," she said, "I'm from Fleckenham, Fleckenham Superior."

"That's a long way to come," said Joss.

"Yes," she said, "but there was a place to be had here and I couldn't wait no longer. There's ten of us at home, you see."

"I see," said Joss. He knew what that meant. "What's your name, miss?"

"Susy," she said, "Susy Rickards. What's yours?"

"My name's Joss Elvin," he said.

"Oh," she said, smiling, and her smile was no longer so shy. "Well, I've told you how I came to be in the wood, but what were you doing here, Mr. Joss?"

"Well," said Joss, and paused to gather courage. "Well, Miss Susy, I work here. I've done all this here. That's my work." He pointed proudly to the clearing, which they had just reached, and his great pile of faggots.

"That's very nice, I'm sure," she said, and smiled again. This time there was mockery in her smile, and not quite knowing what to make of it, Joss walked on in silence to the edge of the wood.

"Now then," he said, when he had carefully handed her across the gate, "you just take that 'aire path through the bushes and through the yard of the owd empty house, and then you're on the road."

"Oh, thank you, Joss," she said. "I don't know what I should ha' done without you."

"But do you know your way back through the wood?" said Joss.

Susy put a finger to her lips and looked at him. "Oh, dear," she said, "I don't know if I do."

"Well, 'haps," said Joss, "—to make sure, I mean—'haps I'd better meet you here and take you back to the other end of the drift."

She nodded gravely. "Yes, 'haps you'd better," she said. Then all at once she smiled, and now there was more than mockery in her smile, something, indeed, that was very near to invitation. "I shan't be long," she said, and with a wave of the hand she ran off down the path.

Joss watched her out of sight among the bushes and then went back to his faggot-pile, but not to work. A girl with a nose like that—he had never seen anything like her, and how she had smiled at him, the look in her eyes! And she would not be long, she had said. It made him quite hot thinking about her, but at the same time he felt a little awed by her unusualness, and it did not occur to him that she might be just as much interested in his person as he was in hers.

Joss well justified his nickname of "the thick 'un." He was square-bodied and stout in the leg, and he had a massive chest on him; but his corduroy trousers and sleeved corduroy waistcoat were trim and well-fitting, and he had a natural ease and agility of movement that tempered the effect of his bulk. His face was square and strong-jawed, but that, too, was tempered by a mild blue eye, by the high colour and the smooth complexion of youth. One glance would have shown a girl that there was nothing in Joss to be afraid of and perhaps a good deal to like, but Joss was not aware of it. All he could think of was how to make himself acceptable to his charmer, and how better than by giving her a gift? Only what gifts were there in Ditch Wood? Joss looked round him anxiously. A maid-servant would not want a faggot, she would not want a gatepost or a rake-handle—but there was that little elm-switch with the knob of root on the end. That would make just the walking-stick for a young lady.

Joss took his hook and chopped the knob to a size that he thought would fit her palm. Then he took out his shut-knife and whittled it smooth. He whittled for nearly half an hour before it seemed smooth enough for so tender a skin, and as he had allowed her only half an hour to get to the village and back, he had to hurry to his post at the end of the drift. But he had been too impatient and he waited a good twenty minutes more before he saw her black straw hat among the bushes.

As soon as she noticed him, she ran the last few steps to the gate with the newspaper under her arm.

"Oh, I'm that glad to see you," she said, as he helped her across. "I couldn't go through that owd wood agin by myself."

Joss cleared his throat and, rather ceremoniously, handed her the walking-stick. "That's for you," he said.

"For me?" she said, examining it curiously. "Oh, I see, for when I'm off on my holiday." She stuck out her elbows and swaggered a little way up the drift with it like a dandy with a cane. Then she stopped and turned round, her face beaming. "That's right a beauty, Joss," she said. "That's just my length."

There was no doubt he had pleased her, and Joss grinned back, congratulating himself on his foresight; but he could not help wondering why she held the stick by the wrong end, and why she looked so hard into his eyes.

"Well, I must now be going," she said, lowering her eyes and turning round again. "Do, I shall be late for tea."

She set out along the drift once more with Joss beside her; but a few yards further on, she stopped and darted off among the nut-stubs.

"Oh, look at the lovely flowers," she cried, and pointed to a long, low bank, white with wood anemones. "Help me to pick some, Joss."

She knelt down on the bank and began to pick with both hands. Joss, who had followed close behind, knelt down at her side and for a moment gazed at the anemones. He had never paid much attention to them before, but now that he saw them against her small, girlish hands, he saw how lovely they were. But Susy's mind was no longer on them. She was looking into his eyes again and all at once she uttered a little scream of pain.

"Oh, the sharp stone!" she cried, and clutching at her knee, she lost her balance and toppled over against him. Joss put out an arm to save her, but she made no attempt to right herself. Indeed, he could feel her body pressing closer against his, he could feel her straw hat crunching on his shoulder, and before he knew where he was, she was right in his arms and they were kissing each other. Now Joss, too, was in danger of losing his balance, and so, still holding her in his arms, he gently lowered her against the bank and stretched himself out beside her. They were hardly settled, however, when Susy sat up with an anxious look.

"I marn't get no mud on my clo'es," she said and pulled her long skirt up above her ankles.

There was no mud, any more than there were sharp stones, on that flowery bank, and Joss, even in his present position, could see that; but he could also see Susy's white cotton stockings above the tops of her coarse leather boots—an intimate and, to him, appealing sight, not often vouchsafed to such as he.

"I marn't get no mud on my clo'es," repeated Susy, and pulled her skirt up right above her knees.

EDGAR CLARY LAID DOWN HIS LONG-HANDLED SLASHER.
He had cut another rod of hedge and it was now time
to sort out the results. The hedge was an old one and
there was plenty of thick stuff and saplings—elm, ash
and maple—to be set aside for poles. Then came the
good small stuff, hazel, ash, elm, now and then a bit
of willow or poplar—which he piled up and tied into
faggots for kindling. Last of all, the worthless stuff, the
dried strings of wild clematis, hops, bryony and other
creepers, the wild rose, thorn and bramble, too prickly
for the chopping-block—this he pulled together into a
heap with a pitchfork and having stuffed a few handfuls
of dry grass under the windward side, set light to it.
There was enough sere wood to make it burn fiercely,
but he watched the flames without satisfaction. He had
already cut several rod of hedge that day. It was nothing new to him and—he looked at his big silver pocket-
watch—there was still more than an hour to go before
tea-time. He was sick of hedging.

Now that his own tool was silent, he could hear the
clack of Joss's hook away at the end of Ditch Wood,
where he, too, was cutting poles and faggots. That was
it, it was just the work for Joss, it was labourer's work.

82

Joss was no longer the thorn in his flesh that he had been; they seldom saw each other now and—out of sight, out of mind. He no longer worried his head if Joss was the better man, for Joss was not there to remind him, and now he could look back with equanimity, and sometimes a little tolerant amusement, to the days when he and Joss had gone about together. They had been all right while their virtue lasted, but he had outgrown them just as he had outgrown Joss; and besides, they were on different levels now, there was no real comparison between them. He understood that now, now that he had taken up with young Fred Akers.

There was not very much difference between the pleasures of a young farmer's son and those of a young labourer. Both of them went drinking and playing games in pubs, both of them ran after girls, both of them liked a bit of sport with a dog or a ferret, or a gun, if they could get hold of one. What made their pleasures seem different was that the farmer's son generally had more money to spend, or at least his father had. Fred Akers had a small pony-trap of his own. He could drive into Brettsleigh whenever he liked and drink in the smarter and more expensive pubs, he could run after the smarter and more expensive girls. He had his own gun too, and could go out shooting at any time, without having to borrow a gun; he could accept an invitation to shoot on some one else's land. Since Edgar had got to know him and had begun to share some of his pleasures, he had awakened to the advantages of being a farmer's son, and he saw no reason why he should not enjoy them like any other.

Unfortunately for Edgar, his father, Walter Clary, was only one generation removed from the peasant. He himself liked to make a good show at Brettsleigh with his black and yellow turn-out, he liked a day's shooting and an evening over a bottle of whisky; but these were the pleasures of a deserving middle age, and he believed in bringing the young up hard. Accordingly Edgar, to his disgust, received no more than a labourer's wages and to his still greater disgust, he did a labourer's work for them. Fred Akers, whose peasant ancestors were more distant than Edgar's, helped his father with the management of the farm. He went to market regularly, he worked in the fields or took a day off when he thought he would. But Edgar was tied to his work. He ploughed and harrowed, he hoed turnips, he carted muck and cut hedges. He was a farmer's son and he did a labourer's work. He was sick of it.

He pulled the scattered embers of his fire together and stuck his pitchfork in the ground. Fred Akers had promised to call for him after tea and they were going in to Brettsleigh Bull, where there was a new and fast-looking barmaid from London. That was something to look forward to, but meanwhile tea was still an hour away and it was time to start on another rod of hedge. He reached for his slasher again to give it a rub, and then looked up as the gate at the corner of the field clattered to. It was Susy, the new maid, of course, coming to fetch his father's newspaper. She looked very neat and demure with her white tucker at the neck and a clean white apron over her brown wincey skirt, and she was swinging a thin little stick with a knob at the end. A starched white apron in such a place was uncommon enough to make any one stare, but as Edgar stared, it did something more to him. She had only been on the farm a week and he had not got very far with her, but here they were, alone in the fields together, here was his chance. He stepped out on the path with his slasher in his hand and waited for her.

"Hullo, Susy," he said banteringly, as she came up and stopped short in front of him. "Arternoon off, eh?"

"I'm going to fetch the master's paper," she replied gravely, and then blushed, as she saw the pointed way he was staring at her apron. Susy knew instinctively what it meant, she had been expecting some such thing of him all the week, and for that very reason, in spite of her blushes, she took care to have a good look at him. The best thing about him was his figure, which was tall, well-proportioned and not too heavy. The next best was perhaps his firm aquiline nose, but the rest of his features were pale and colourless, like his pale-blue eyes and his pale, strawy hair. By comparison with Joss there was not much sign of warmth in him.

"A nice life you gals have," said Edgar, continuing his banter. "Clean white aprons and a nice country walk afore tea."

Susy giggled. "I was up afore you this morning," she said.

"Oh, were you?" he said. "Well, where did you get your little owd stick from?"

Susy blushed. "I picked that up in the stackyard," she said.

"Oh, you did, did you?" Edgar looked at her suspiciously; he knew there were no such sticks lying about in the stackyard. "I'll cut you a better stick'n that out of the fence," he said.

"I don't want that, thank you, Master Edgar," she replied stiffly. "I must now be a-going."

Since Edgar was planted in the pathway, she started to sidle round him, but before she had taken two steps, he caught his arm round her waist and pulled her back.

"You marn't be so short with me, Susy," he said. "You ain't half a bad gal, you know."

"Oh, let me go, Master Edgar," she said, tugging at his wrist. "Do, I shall be late with the master's paper."

"I shan't let you go till you give me a kiss, Susy," he said, grinning and showing his teeth.

"Oh, no, Master Edgar," she cried, tugging harder. "Please, Master Edgar—Joss Elvin'll see us." With a sudden wrench she broke his grip and flung herself away from him.

The grin left Edgar's face and he stared for a moment as she backed away from him. "So that's who that is?" he said.

Susy's face went crimson. "I never said no such thing," she cried, and turning her back on him, she ran off down the path.

"Now I know who cut you that little owd stick," he shouted after her.

"No, you don't," she called back over her shoulder.

"That was Joss Elvin," he shouted, but this time Susy did not answer and ran on without turning her head.

Edgar stood quite still, watching her white apron twinkle against the brown ploughland. He saw her, after about fifty yards, glance quickly backwards and drop into a walk. He saw her walk up to the edge of the wood, he saw her disappear up the drift, and then all at once he could no longer hear the clack of Joss's hook.

Edgar bit his lip and turning to the hedge again, let fly with his slasher. It was bad enough to want a girl and then have her taken away from you—taken away even before you had wanted her. That made him want her all the more, so much that it hurt not to have her. What was worse, however, it was Joss, his own father's labourer, who had taken her away, and still worse than that, the girl belonged to the house, she was his by right. Out of sight, out of mind, eh? It was theft, just like the theft of those sandwiches, and it was more than he could endure. Whole saplings fell on his head, whippy branches lashed his cheek and thorns tore at his hands, as he blindly hacked, but he still hacked away. At every stroke he cut Joss down, but Joss as many times stood up again.

An hour passed and Edgar was beginning to feel better. He had gone on hacking at the hedge till he could hack no more, but in doing so, he had sweated some of the heat and turmoil out of his mind. He could think now and a cool determination had taken the place of his rage. He was going to show Joss and whatever it cost him—he had reckoned it all up—he was going to pay Joss out. They would see who was the better man now.

It was nearly time to knock off and he had already stopped cutting, but he still lingered by his hedge, crouching in a position from which he could see the end of the wood without being seen. Then after a few minutes things happened as he had expected. Susy appeared at the end of the drift, stopped, and looked fixedly in his direction. She was looking for him, he knew, and she was making up her mind whether to slip round through the adjacent fields to avoid him. But Susy, reassured by seeing nothing of him, set off along the path she had come by and he squatted back to wait for her. It was not long before he could hear her hurrying footsteps and a jaunty little tune she was humming in time with them. Then her white apron became visible through the bushes and he stepped out in front of her.

"Oh," she said with a start, and then regarding him with dismay. "You wholly made me jump."

"I'm sorry, Susy," said Edgar in his gentlest voice. "I didn't mean to. But there's suthun I meant to tell you."

"Oh?" she said doubtingly, and began to edge away.

"Don't you be afraid, Susy," he said, smiling and making no move to stop her. "I ain't a-coming for you.

88

But you know, just now when you came past—I—I didn't mean no harm. I mean suthun else. I—I think the world of you, Susy."

His voice had grown quite husky and Susy looked hard at him.

"Ah," she said, looking down and fidgeting at a clod with the toe of her boot, "you don't only say that."

"Oh, don't I?" said Edgar in an injured tone. "Well, do you listen here, Susy. I want to arst you suthun. Have Joss ever arst you to walk out with him?"

Susy did not answer, but went on fidgeting with the clod.

"But have he?" insisted Edgar.

"Er—well—no, he hain't," she murmured, without looking up.

Edgar drew a deep breath before he took the next step. "What I mean to say," he said, and coughed. "What I mean to say, 'haps we might walk out together to-night like?"

Susy raised her eyes at last and stared at him wonderingly. But she had not said no, and Edgar pressed his suit.

"Then we could go to Church next Sunday," he said, "and that'll soon be the Brettsleigh Easter Fair, and I don't want to go alone."

Susy still stared at him, and then twitched her lips in a half-smile. "What ever would your father say?" she asked.

Edgar smiled too, for his father was his trumpcard.

"I shall tell him we're walking out reg'lar," he said,

"and then he can't say nothen. You see, he've only got me to leave the farm to," he added significantly.

Susy opened her eyes wide and then giggled, wavering.

"I don't know, I'm sure," she said.

"I tell you what," said Edgar eagerly. "He's now on his way back from market, that's just his time. So we'll now go down and meet him, and tell him right afore tea."

"Oh, no," she said, shrinking back, "I shouldn't care for that."

"Don't you worry," said Edgar. "He 'on't say nothen, and I want you to see I'm all fair and square with you. Don't you believe that, Susy?"

Susy smiled quite graciously. "Yes, I believe that, Edgar," she said.

"Well, come along, my duck," he said, and having shouldered his slasher, he slipped his arm through hers. "You'll come, 'on't you?"

"Well, I don't mind," she said, and then hung back, as he faced her round to the wood again. "But I ain't a-going through there," she said.

"Don't you fret, we ain't," said Edgar, giving her arm a squeeze. "There's a path right round the wood."

"Oh, I see," she said trustingly, and let him carry her off.

Edgar took another deep breath and breathed it noisily out. He had hardly expected to win this last point so easily, but it was to him the point that mattered most. He knew, and she luckily seemed to have forgotten, that Joss, too, would be knocking off now, and would soon be on his way through the wood to Chaffinch's. But there was no time to spare and this, their first walk out together, was no lover's stroll. There was no time for conversation, no time for caresses or endearments.

"We marn't dawdle," he said, thrusting her on. "Father drive fast and I don't want to miss him."

It could not have been better timed, for when, having skirted the wood, they reached the further end of the drift, where the path led down to Chaffinch's, he heard some one whistling, and glancing over his shoulder, he saw Joss walking down the drift barely thirty yards behind them. Susy, too, turned to glance, but she hastily turned round again. She clutched Edgar's arm tight and tried to hurry him on, red to the ears and sinking her head to her breast to hide it. But Edgar was in no hurry now and deliberately held her back. He put his arm right round her waist and turned round again, and more than once, to make sure that Joss could see them. He squared his shoulders and his walk became involuntarily something of a strut. He had waited a long time for this moment; he was the better man at last.

Edgar's luck was in that day, for after a few minutes of this triumphal progress, they came out through the yard of Chaffinch's to the road, and there was Walter Clary's black and yellow dogcart, bearing down on them at a fast trot. It was beautifully timed, he thought, as he stood by the yard gate with one arm round Susy's waist and the other raised to catch his father's eye.

"Hullo, what the—what are you two doing there like

that?" demanded Walter Clary, as he pulled up beside them. He had had several whiskies in Brettsleigh and was not quite certain of the things his eyes saw.

Edgar held Susy tight and tried to look like a dutiful son. "I wanted to tell you, Father," he said. "Me and Susy are walking out."

"Oh, you are, are you?" Walter Clary's chin jerked backwards in surprise. "Well, well," he went on, stroking his beard in a bewildered fashion, "I don't know, I'm sure. I never was a proud man. I don't care if she is in sarvice so long as she make you a good wife. But I didn't come here to jow to you, together. Have Joss gone home, d' you know?"

"I don't rightly know," said Edgar, and for the third time he took a deep breath. He had been wondering all along how his father would take it.

"Well, I hope he hain't," said Walter Clary. "I've driv hard all the way from Brettsleigh to get hold of him. Ah, there he is, just a-coming into the yard. Come on, up you get, both of you. I'll give you a lift home." He leapt down from the trap, handed the reins to Edgar, and strode into the yard.

"Hey, Joss," he cried, "I want you."

Joss, who had halted by the back gate and was watching Susy and Edgar climb into the trap, came reluctantly forward.

"I've got suthun to tell you, Joss," said Walter Clary. "I seed Tod Jordan at Brettsleigh to-day and he say he can't finish Ditch Wood this winter. So you're a-coming back along o' me to-morrow morning."

"Well, I ain't," replied Joss sullenly.

"What's that?" said Walter Clary. "I tell you, I've settled all that along o' Tod."

"Well, I tell you I ain't a-coming," repeated Joss.

"Well, of all the—what d'you mean, you young bastard?" cried Walter Clary.

"I don't want no more of Overham, I'm a-going to London," said Joss, and turning round, he walked slowly back towards the wood.

"Well, I'll go to hell!" said Walter Clary.

JOSS LEANT UP AGAINST THE LAMP-POST AND GAZED across the street at the house opposite. Its main shell was a typical square box of Victorian yellow brick; the stucco facings that adorned its doors and windows were in the Gothic style, and the solid pediment that concealed its slates, but not the crooked phalanx of cowls and chimneypots above them, was of flowing baroque elegance. In the middle of this pediment, immediately below the classical funerary urn that crowned it, was engraved the following inscription:

THE INKERMAN

1863

The details of this frowzy, soot-begrimed architecture were of no account to Joss. To him it was just a house, a house in a street, and Joss was not used to streets. To be sure, this street was another world to the Bow Road just round the corner, where the never-ending procession of gaudy horse-buses, dashing hansoms, crawling market waggons, drays, tradesmen's carts, costers' barrows—in fact, everything on wheels conceivable—was something to dazzle the eye, even an eye that had seen Brettsleigh High Street in fair-time. It was a great relief to be clear of the noise, the elbows that prodded your ribs, the feet that trod on your toes, the wheels that threatened to crush all your bones; but even the quiet back street was no less unfamiliar. It was not so much the strangeness of its architecture, strange though it was, that made the place so unfamiliar, as the vast urban landscape of bricks and mortar and chimneypots. Even in Brettsleigh High Street you had only to look up to see the green hilltops that overhung it or the elm-trees by the churchyard. But here, wherever you looked, there was no escape from the chimneypots, there was not a tree, a blade of grass. It gave Joss the uncomfortable feeling of being hemmed in, of being trapped, almost; and instinct prevailing, he badly wanted to run away. But only for a moment. He had not come to London to run away.

Outside the public-house three pale, middle-aged women with black shawls over their shoulders and steel curlers in their hair were drinking stout, and a fourth, similarly attired, was trying to persuade a pale, shrunken baby in a battered perambulator to take a sip from her pony-glass of gin. Joss stared at them, but it was not so much the strangeness of their clothes or the sight of a baby drinking gin that made him stare, as the paleness of their faces, which by contrast revealed to him the colour—the pink, the red, the purple, the bronze—that he had never before noticed in the country faces of Overham and Brettsleigh, the only faces he had so far known. Those were real faces, but these—these were like plants that had been left in a dark cellar.

While he was digesting this phenomenon, another one came into view. It was a creature approaching along the pavement who, though he undoubtedly was a man, somehow did not look like a man, and it took Joss several moments of staring to realize that this was because he had no nose. It was preposterous, but he had no nose. The man himself, however, seemed quite unconscious of its absence. He nodded unconcernedly to the four women and they no less unconcernedly returned his nod; they were more interested in the baby and its apparent distaste for gin. Joss could no longer contain his curiosity and crossed the road to the group.

"Excuse me, together," he said, "but who was that 'aire?"

"What, 'im?" said the woman with the baby. "Why, 'im, we calls 'im Nobby."

"But he've got no nose," said Joss incredulously.

The four women laughed uproariously; it seemed a great joke to them. "You look arter your own, mate," said one of the stout-drinkers, "and keep away from the skirts."

"Who are you anyway?" said the women with the baby.

"My name's Joss Elvin," said Joss boldly—that was a real fact, there was nothing doubtful about that—"and I'm looking for Mr. Alf Summers."

"Well, you'll find him in there be'ind the counter," said the woman, pointing to a pair of swing doors labelled "Public Bar." "Mine's a large gin, deary," she cackled, as Joss plunged eagerly between them.

96

Alf Summers was grossly fat. He was so fat that, collarless and stripped to his shirtsleeves, he reclined against, rather than sat upon, his high wooden stool behind the counter, and the greater part of his features seemed to have merged into the general mass of his huge egg of a head. A dark, greasy quiff and a dark, pendulous moustache were its only notable excrescences.

"What's your order?" he demanded, as soon as he caught sight of Joss, and reached for the beer-pulls.

"Are you Mr. Alf Summers?" inquired Joss politely.

"Yes, I am," said the landlord. "Watcher want?"

"If you please," said Joss, "Mr. Wolff, Mr. Iky Wolff, said you might be wanting a potman."

Alf Summers looked him up and down. He pursed and unpursed his lips, he scratched his quiff.

"Well, I don't know," he said. " 'Ere I've been without a potman a month now—the bleeders won't stay. But Christ, you're one of the thickest damn' blokes I ever see!"

Startled by this sudden apostrophe, Joss breathed in hard, which filled out his chest and made him look thicker still.

"But any fool can dror beer," continued the landlord. "Do you know that, young feller? What I want is somebody as can chuck the rowdies out and keep the peelers away. I used to do it myself but I'm getting beyond it now. Do you think you can do it, young feller?"

Joss grinned, and in a gesture of embarrassment put one of his large brown hands on the counter.

"Blimey," exclaimed the landlord, "there's a bloody

97

great paw for you! Here, m'lad, I'll give you a week's trial, fifteen bob a week and all found. Come along in, do."

He lifted up a flap in the counter and pulled Joss in by his coat-skirts.

"Now then," he went on, when the flap was down again and Joss behind the beer-engine, "you can get right to work now. I reckon a bloke as big as you knows the price of beer all right. But there's one thing more, young feller. Come along 'ere a minute." He drew Joss over to a glass door at the back of the bar.

"D'you see them two there?" he said, pointing to two large women seated at a table in the room beyond with a cribbage-board between them. "Well, they're my missis and daughter, and you ain't to give the bitches no beer. They'll arst you for it, but don't give the bitches a drop, not a bloody drop. D'you 'ear?"

Joss grinned and nodded.

"Well, now, we're all ready to start, and first thing you do, you can dror me a nice pint of beer with a nice 'ead on it."

Dusk was coming on and as the evening customers trickled in, Joss was kept busy drawing pints, including one every half-hour for the landlord, opening bottles of stout, and serving nips of gin and whisky. To a man accustomed to heavy labour with his hands it hardly seemed like work at all, and since beer had for some time been one of his principal pleasures, it was a pleasure also to handle it. He had that mingled sense of satisfaction and command that he had often had at plough or making a rick or loading a hay-waggon, when everything was going well, and he was not even disconcerted at being openly discussed and pointed out as "Alf's new potman." He was enjoying himself.

After about an hour and a half the pints the landlord had drunk began to assert themselves and he waddled slowly out into the yard. The yard door had hardly closed on him when the glass door behind the bar opened and a great lumpy girl, built on the same lines as Alf Summers himself, but not yet so featureless, poked her head round it.

"Potman, potman," she called in a loud whisper, "fill the jug, will you?" She thrust a three-pint jug into one of his hands and a two-shilling piece into the other.

"But—but, ma'am—" began Joss, recalling the landlord's first injunction.

"Don't you worry about him," said the girl, patting him on the shoulder. "Just you fill it up, and you can keep the change for yourself—every night, potman. Go on, before he comes back."

Joss hardly knew where he stood. He had scruples about deceiving his new master, but at the same time he did not want to offend the women of the house, and it certainly seemed a pity that they should go without their beer. However, he had no time now for settling nice moral issues and until he had, this once would do no harm; so he hurriedly filled the jug.

The girl's eyes gloated as she took it from him. "That's

the ticket," she said. "I should keep the lot if I were you."

Just as Joss was pocketing the two-shilling piece, there was a scuffle among a little group on the other side of the counter and a woman screamed. Joss was not in time to see what had happened, but this sort of thing, he remembered, was what he was here to stop, and he brought the flat of his hand down on the mahogany with a smack that upset several of the smaller mugs and glasses on it.

"Hey there," he shouted, "that's enow."

A neatly dressed young woman with a flower-trimmed hat, who was standing just opposite him with a glass of stout, shook her head warningly.

"Leave him alone," she said, in a low voice. "He's a bruiser, he is. Fights on the halls."

At the same time a man turned round from the scuffling group and faced Joss. He was dressed in a scalloped jacket and bell-bottomed trousers of some black stuff with a finish like watered silk. He was short but powerfully built; he had a crushed nose and cauliflower ears, and a defiant lock of hair over one eye. He certainly looked as if he might be a bruiser.

"You mind your own business," he shouted, and turning round, he struck a meek-faced little woman across the mouth, on which a small gout of blood was already forming.

Joss threw up the flap and stepped out in front of the counter. "Come along, together," he said quietly. "You marn't act like that in here."

The man in the black suit turned round again and took up a threatening stand. "Oh, we marn't, marn't we?" he jeered, mimicking Joss's Suffolk. "Where do you come from, cully?"

Joss suddenly went red in the face. "You can arst that when I've finished with you," he said, and advanced on the jeerer, who was already putting up his fists.

Joss knew nothing about boxing—indeed, he did not even see the situation as a problem in pugilistics. His business was to remove the man from the bar and as he set about it, the appropriate rustic image presented itself to his mind. The bar was Walter Clary's barn; the man was a coomb sack of wheat, and outside was one of Walter Clary's waggons, waiting to receive it. He acted accordingly.

The man led with his left in proper boxing fashion, but Joss made no attempt to counter the blow. He just seized the lunging fist with both his hands and swung the man bodily round behind him. Then, letting go with one hand, he seized the man by the slack of his trousers and methodically hoisted him on to the small of his back like the coomb of wheat he imagined him to be. The man's free arm flailed desperately over Joss's head, but since he was firmly spreadeagled, back to Joss's back, he could do no damage, and when Joss had got his burden comfortable, he proceeded to carry it through the swing doors, which he pushed open with his own head. Outside in the street there was no farm waggon, but, as it happened, an empty coster's barrow, and into that, with a quick stoop, he shot his coomb of wheat.

"Now where do I come from?" he said, as he watched the barrow up-end with the impact and topple over sideways.

The first person he met when he turned back into the bar was the meek-faced little woman; but she no longer looked so meek. She had become a raging termagant.

"I'll larn yer," she cried. "I'll larn yer to knock my hubby abaht. I'll scratch yer bloody eyes aht, I will."

This time another rustic image presented itself to Joss. He was in Ditch Wood and the woman was a faggot, just tied and waiting to be carried over to the pile. It was not difficult to duck out of the range of her nails, and then, seizing her by the back of her waistband and the collar of her jacket, he carried her face downwards into the street, where he dropped her on top of her still prostrate husband.

The bar was quite hushed when he entered again, and as he walked up to the counter, the company respectfully made way for him. Alf Summers was back on his stool by now, blinking hard and gasping a little. When he had recovered his breath, he waddled across to Joss and gripped his arm.

"Listen to me, young feller," he said. "Your week's trial's over. You're took on, pound a week and all found —d'you 'ear?"

Two customers now walked up to the counter and rapped for the potman.

"What'll you 'ave?" they said simultaneously.

ALF SUMMERS PICKED UP HIS LARGE GLASS GOBLET OF rum and tea and gulped it noisily.

" 'Ere, Joss," he said, when he had set it down empty, " 'ave another bit of 'am."

Joss looked up at the liver-and-white china spaniels on the plush-draped mantel-shelf and sighed.

"No, thank you all the same," he said. He could not have swallowed another morsel.

Alf Summers snorted and cut himself another plateful. "You don't seem to 'ave much of an appetite," he said, "not for a country clod'opper. Now look at me. I can allus eat another slice of 'am."

Joss looked at him and marvelled. He had never seen such quantities of food on a table. There was not only meat every day, there was meat three or four times a day. Even now, at tea-time, there was a choice of ham, sausage rolls, cheese, fish-paste, jam and seed-cake. And all this display of food was not intended as a mere titillation of the palate. It was there to be eaten, and the Summers family took full advantage of it. Outside the farmyard, Joss had never seen such meals eaten, and between meals they all three maintained themselves with constant snacks of bread and cheese and pickles or slices of bread and jam; except when they were drinking or sleeping, it seemed, they were always eating. Alf Summers and his wife were originally migrants from the country and, like his parents, had been born in the "hungry forties," so that it might have been supposed that they were making up for past privations. But their daughter, Levina, had no such excuse. Encouraged by their example, she just ate for eating's sake and already, at twenty-four, she was on the way to becoming as gross and lethargic as her father.

When he had cleared up his second plateful of ham and drained his rummer a second time, Alf Summers wiped his mouth on the back of his hand and pushed his high wooden armchair away from the table.

"Listen to me, Joss," he said. "I reckon you'd better 'ave your night off to-night, and I'll tell you for why. Customers, you see, get paid Friday night. Saturday morning children go and get the Sunday clo'es out of pawn, mother gets the Sunday dinner. Well, then Saturday night they starts to drink—if they ain't started Friday—and goes on all Sunday and Sunday night. Them as 'as anything left goes on till Monday night. You knows all that. You've just been through it."

Joss grinned and gently rubbed a small lump above his eye.

"Well, you see," continued Alf Summers, "to-day's Toosday and the wages are all spent. The Sunday clo'es are back at uncle's till Saturday to keep 'em through the week, and there ain't no money left for beer till Friday again; so we shall be pretty quiet to-night and I can manage 'em all right by myself. Off you go then. Don't come home drunk, and keep off the skirts. I'm going to have forty winks now till opening-time. Be off with you."

He settled himself back in his armchair with a newspaper over his face. Levina made room among the dirty plates and cups for the cribbage-board and handed a worn pack of cards to her mother.

"Cut for deal," she said.

There was certainly nothing to stay for.

Joss was wearing his best corduroy trousers, his Sunday coat of dark-grey "stable" tweed and a neckerchief of fine shepherd's-plaid check; but he did not feel at all conspicuous as he walked out into the Bow Road. Corduroys were still worn by town working men and the white collar was still far from being universal. Except for his ruddy-brown cheeks, there were plenty like him in the Bow Road; and now, after a week at The Inkerman, as he had occasion to observe, the Bow Road itself was no longer so strange and terrifying. During that week he had stopped a score of fights and had two himself; he had "chucked out" more drunks, both male and female, than he could remember, he had taken more money over the counter than he dared to think of. In fact, he had made himself indispensable and he was in complete command of The Inkerman public bar, in more senses than one.

Alf Summers, he had discovered, had two cantankerous periods during the day, when the effects of the alcohol he had last drunk were wearing off and the alcohol he was starting to drink had not yet produced any. During these periods, which coincided roughly with the morning and evening opening-times, he was troubled with the illusion that his wife and daughter drank more than he did—which was far from being the case—and forbade them all access to the bar. If they had had the patience to wait until intoxication had improved his temper, they could have had all the beer they wanted for nothing; but cribbage was evidently a dry game and they preferred to give Joss a two-shilling piece—previously extracted from the till—to have their three-pint jug filled when they wanted it. For Joss there was no longer any moral issue. He sympathized with their thirst and accordingly pocketed the money every night. He did not care for the smell of his bedroom, nor for the bugs that a warm April was luring from his bed; but a pound a week and all found with a regular fourteen shillings a week from the women and other tips from generous customers, with more food than he could eat and more beer than he could drink—that was better than ten or twelve bob a week on the land. He was a man of the world now.

He was a man of the world, and looking back, he found it difficult to believe that only ten days ago he had left Overham with a wounded heart, a heart jealous and resentful too, but above all wounded beyond repair. Susy had been a creature so new to him, so fresh and entrancing, her embraces so ardent, spontaneous and unrestrained, and the austere early-spring charm of Ditch

Wood so perfectly attuned to them, that he could not but regard those seven days, those seven half-hours rather, that he had spent with her, as the rarest, the most beautiful, episode of his life, one that was never likely to be surpassed. The emotions it had given birth to had come after the episode was ended, because it had ended. They had made him suffer as he had never suffered, they had driven him headlong from Overham; but now, as he walked along the Bow Road and looked back on the pangs of his jealousy and disappointed passion, they appeared in a different light. Susy had made no vows of fidelity, she had not even owned to loving him; and she had a right to do as she liked. What she had done—although it was a thing he would not have done himself—only proved his own folly in imagining too much, in expecting more than was offered; and even if it robbed her of qualities that his doting imagination had created, it could not rob their episode of its essential sweetness.

Even his first blind hatred of Edgar had given way to a cooler, more logical aversion. Edgar's insistence in parading his triumph told its own tale. If Joss had been one to put two and two together, to read minds and seek for motives, it might have explained the whole of their uneasy relationship; but even without that it told him enough. It told him that Edgar had wanted to score off him, and also, a thing he had for long half known, that he himself thoroughly disliked Edgar. It was no good being sentimental over the time when they had been "mates." That meant nothing. Edgar had been grudging and unresponsive and cross-grained even then; and now he not only considered himself too good for his old mate, but he had tried to score off him—and had succeeded. As Daddy Haines had once said, he had no heart, "not for ship, nit for nothen else." Joss no longer hated him as a few days ago he had done. Now he shrank from him rather, as something alien and unsympathetic by nature, something that he wanted out of sight and out of mind, out of his life altogether.

Doubtless, it was not necessary to come to London to get away from Edgar. It would have been enough to go as far as the next farm, the next village. But a wounded heart could seldom have been healed, or a turbulent mind restored to reasonableness and tranquillity, more quickly than Joss's at The Inkerman. There were at least as many interesting things to look at in the outside world as in Ditch Wood and he was already at home in that world. He was not yet ready to admit that it could bear comparison with Overham or Brettsleigh, and he still regarded its blanched denizens with something like the amazed contempt of a noble redskin visiting the paleface; they even needed a man from Overham to keep them in order. Neverthless he enjoyed keeping them in order, he could not help it, just as much as he enjoyed ministering to their pleasures, which he was frequently called upon to share; and since all this was what he was paid for, life at The Inkerman seemed to hold out the prospect of a continuous beano.

To Joss the Bow Road of the nineties was a free show. There were Italian organ-grinders with monkeys on chains and German brass bands playing in the street.

Mustachio'd soldiers in pill-box hats and scarlet bum-freezers, bearded and caftaned Polish Jews from White-chapel and coloured seamen from the India Docks rubbed shoulders on the pavement. There was a man who sold hot baked potatoes from a large black oven with brass knobs and a halo of raw potatoes impaled on spikes round the door; he gave you a hot potato, a pinch of salt and a piece of paper to wrap them in for a half-penny. There were sellers of roast chestnuts, cockles and jellied eels. There was an old man crouching in the gutter and extracting music from a tin whistle with one of his nostrils. A cripple slithered by on one hand and one buttock. A Transylvanian peasant in top boots and a small boy beating a drum were putting a huge "danc-ing" bear through its pathetic, shambling paces.

Joss drank it all in avidly and although the show was free, he could not resist giving pennies to all the per-formers he passed, or sampling the cockles, the jellied eels and the potatoes. Then, just as he was beginning to feel tired from all this unaccustomed bustle and excite-ment, he found himself in front of a big red-brick build-ing with a notice in unmistakable capitals over the door, which said:

ENTER IN YE WEARY AND REST.
ALL WELCOME.

Taking the notice at its word, Joss pushed open the door and stepped into a large dim hall, full, as far as he could see in the dimness, of hard wooden chairs. This was not what he had bargained for, but before he could withdraw, a blue-uniformed official seized him by the arm and ushered him to one of the chairs. At the other end of the hall, on a low platform, a brawny man in a scarlet jersey was addressing himself directly, it seemed, to Joss.

"Yes, my friends," he bawled, in ripe East-end cockney, "I was earning good wages as a stevedore, but I 'ad the devil in my 'eart. I used to sing worldly songs and frequent public 'ouses. In them dens of iniquity I often used to get drunk. I wasted my money, I quarrelled and fought, I neglected my family, and, shame on me!"—he raised a hand in the air and smote the breast of his scarlet jersey—"I thrashed my wife. I 'ad become like a beast, my brethren, I 'ad taken a first-class ticket, by express, to 'ell."

Then he clasped his hands and his voice became low and husky.

"Brethren," he went on, "I should be in 'ell now if it 'adn't been for the Salvation Army. They found me one night, drunk and bleeding in the gutter. They took me up and cared for me. They told me of Jesus and the blood of the Lamb. Brethren, my 'ole life was changed. I put away all evil things. I lived good and clean, I give up drink and fighting, I 'anded my wife my wages every week.

"Oh, my brethren," he went on in a shaking voice, "'ow can I tell you of the peace in my 'eart now my eyes are fixed on my 'eavenly 'ope, the Lamb? Brethren, my brethren, I am saved!" His voice ascended to an ecstatic scream and he collapsed on his knees.

As his speech ended, several people in the body of the hall leapt to their feet and echoed his last words in the same ecstatic scream. "I am saved, I am saved!"

Before the cries had died away, another man in a scarlet jersey mounted the platform and gave testimony. He was not so eloquent as the first, who was evidently a star turn; but his testimony was on the same lines. He had spent his money on riotous living, he had drunk, fought and gambled, and beaten his wife. Then one day the Salvation Army had found him and delivered him from hell. He was saved. There were more ecstatic cries, and then a third sinner followed with a similar story, and after him a fourth.

Joss began to feel uncomfortable. He, too, frequented public houses, and not only that, he was employed in one. He, too, had been drunk in his time; he had sung numerous worldly songs and he had recently started fighting. The only sin he had not committed, it seemed, was that of wife-beating, but even so, there was no doubt that he had committed enough to put him in serious danger of hell-fire. Just as he reached this conclusion, there were more shouts of "I am saved!" immediately in front of him and his head began to go round; he began to wonder if he was drunk or sober. Then the official who had shown him to his seat came up and whispered in his ear.

"Brother," he whispered, "brother, are you saved?"

Joss's head went round so fast that it suddenly seemed to explode.

"I am saved, I am saved!" he shouted, as ecstatically

as any of them, and then sank back in his chair with tears streaming from his eyes.

The official put his hand on Joss's shoulder. "Praised be the Lord!" he announced to the congregation. "Our brother is saved."

The congregation turned round and stared at Joss. "Praised be the Lord!" they cried.

Joss's head suddenly stopped going round. The ecstasy had passed, and all he was conscious of was that he was being stared at for making a fool of himself and blubbering like a kid. He felt uncomfortable again, more uncomfortable than ever, as the official continued to stand by him, patting his shoulder and repeating, over and over again, "Praised be the Lord!"

At the other end of the hall another official was now reciting the words of a hymn and when he had finished, the harmonium struck up a tune that to Joss seemed oddly familiar.

"Why, blast," he exclaimed, "if that ain't *The Young Sailor Cut Down in His Prime!*"

"Perhaps, brother," replied the official at his side very suavely, "but why should the devil have all the best tunes?"

Joss stared at him and then stood up from his chair. He had really come to himself now; he knew there was nothing to do with the devil about *The Young Sailor*; it was his father's song. He no longer cared a snap for hell-fire.

"Where are you going, brother?" said the official in surprise.

"I'm going out to have a wet," said Joss defiantly, all his natural paganism reasserting itself.

"But you said you were saved," protested the official.

"Well, I made a mistake," said Joss. "Please let me out."

The official pulled back the door and raised his hand with the solemn wrath of a priest excommunicating the heretic. "Get you from us," he cried, "miserable sinner!"

As Joss lumbered out into the fresh air, his head started to go round again, so fast that he shut his eyes and clutched at the air for support. When he opened his eyes again, he perceived, to his relief, that he had not clutched in vain. Somebody was holding his elbow, somebody was talking to him, and the voice was a woman's.

"You silly boy," she was saying, "to go into a place like that—all hot and dark, and all that screaming and singing. It's enough to make you giddy."

Joss turned and looked at her. She was neatly dressed in a dark-blue coat and skirt with a perky, flower-trimmed hat on top; and she had a plump smiling face that he somehow seemed to remember. He liked the look of her; but what he wanted now was a drink.

"Beg your pardon, miss," he said, "would you show me the way to the nearest public?"

"That's just what I'm going to do," she said. "It's set quite handy for the likes of you."

She took a firm hold of his arm and guided him solicitously, as if he had been a blind man or an invalid, to a building a few steps further on that might easily have been mistaken for The Inkerman, except that the inscription on its pediment was "The Cross Keys." Here she pushed him into an empty, dark and cosy private bar and, with undiminished solicitude, settled him in a corner seat.

"Now what'd you like?" she said.

"A nice pint's what I want," said Joss, "but look here, miss, what are you having? I'm getting the drinks."

"Oh, no, you aren't," she replied firmly. "I'm treating you, so just you sit still."

In a minute or two she was back with a bottle of stout for herself and the pint of mild, which, still maintaining the fiction of the blind man or the invalid, she carefully placed in his hands. Joss did not even wait to wish her good health, but drank greedily, to the bottom of the mug.

"Ah, that's better," he breathed, smacking his lips. "I wanted that."

"Let me get you another," said the young woman.

"No, that's my turn," protested Joss, but vainly. She pushed him back in his seat and carried his mug to the counter again. "I tell you, I'm treating you," she said, as she brought it back full. "Go on, drink that up."

Joss took a good pull at it and wiped the froth off his lips with a forefinger. "You know, miss," he said, "I reckon that was suthun I'd ate that made me come over like that. I wholly felt funny inside."

"And no wonder," she scolded, "after all those cockles and jellied eels and taters you've been scoffing."

Joss looked hard at her. "Why, that's just what I did have," he said, "but how did you know, miss?"

"My name's not 'miss,' it's Hetty," she said, "and how did I know? Well, I've followed you half the length of the Bow Road, so I couldn't help it, could I?"

Joss looked at her harder still. "Followed me half the length of the Bow Road?" he repeated slowly, and then grinned. "Well, blast me if that ain't a master bit! But fare to me somehow, I know your face."

Hetty smiled appreciatively. "I shouldn't be surprised if you do," she said, "but anyhow I know all about you, Mr. Joss Elvin."

"You do?" exclaimed Joss.

"Yes, you're potman at The Inkerman, and I saw you throw that filthy bruiser and his tart out of the bar a week ago."

"Well, blast," said Joss again, "now I know who you are. That was you told me to keep off him 'cause he was a professional."

"That's right," said Hetty eagerly, "and you didn't do what you were told. But—but weren't you wonderful? The way you picked 'em up, just like feather pillows!" She turned her head away, grown suddenly bashful, and lowered her eyes. "I couldn't sleep that night," she said, "for thinking of it."

"Oh?" said Joss over-hastily, "I'm sorry to hear that."

"Oh, but I wasn't sorry," replied Hetty, turning back to him, bright-eyed. "Only, you see, that was my night off and I didn't get another till tonight, and when I went round to The Inkerman, I found it was your night off too."

"Oh?" said Joss, and grinned. The implications of her sleepless night had now dawned on him.

"Yes," continued Hetty with a mock-rueful look, "I know you don't mind, but think of poor me. And then, just as I was going home to bed, I saw you in the Bow Road. I saw you give the man with the monkey a penny. I saw you eat all those jellied eels and things. I saw you look after all the girls." She nudged him. "Oh, yes, I did, and I was just going to say how-d'ye-do to you when you went off into that psalm-smiter place; so I followed you in."

"Did you, by God?" said Joss with a start. "And so you saw—?"

"Yes, I did," she said, nudging him again, "and, my, didn't you act funny? But it was lucky I was there, wasn't it, when you went all giddy like."

Joss grinned. "You know, Hetty—" he said, and stopped.

"Yes?" Her voice was encouraging.

"Well, I think you're half tidy," he said.

"What say?" and taking his Suffolk too literally, she frowned.

"I mean," Joss hurried on, "I mean you're just the sort of gal I like."

The cloud lifted from her face. "Do you think so?" she said, and pushed up close to him, groping for his hand.

"Yes, I do," said Joss with conviction, as their fingers

met. "You see, miss—I mean, Hetty—I'm fresh up from the country and I don't know my way about."

"Well, I'll show you round a bit," she said with a significant smile, and then, after a glance to make sure there was no one at the counter, she held her face up to him.

"Kiss me, deary," she said.

The kiss took Joss's breath away, not only by its warmth and softness, but also by its calculated, languorous sensuality. No country girl, not even Susy, had ever kissed him like that. But it did not last long, for the landlord came back to their part of the counter and Hetty drew away.

"What a nuisance he is!" she said, pouting with disgust. "But I tell you what, Joss." Her face lit up and she impatiently caught his arm. "You see, I'm a skivvy at a draper's down the road and my missis is out for the evening. So let's go along to my bedroom. It's round at the back, in the basement. Nobody 'll see us go and missis won't be back till eleven. We can have it all to ourselves." She pulled at his arm and there was no mistaking the look in her eyes. "Besides, we can take a bottle of beer along with us," she added. "What do you say, Joss?"

Once again Joss's breath was taken from him. He had never met such a girl. She needed no running after—it was she who had run after him—nor any coaxing for a kiss—she had demanded it. And now, without any beating about the bush, without any false modesty, she had invited him home—to her bedroom. She knew just what she wanted, and what he wanted too, no nonsense about her. What was more, what no other girl had ever done for him, she had already treated him to two pints of beer. He could not help grinning at the thought of his luck; for even beyond the doors of The Inkerman the beano still went on. He was glad he had come to town.

"That's right," said Hetty, promptly taking his grin for an answer. "I believe in having a bit of fun while you've got the chance."

"So do I," said Joss.

THE GREEN AND ORANGE HORSE-BUS JOLTED UP TO ITS Tottenham Court Road stop and Joss clambered down the narrow stairs into Oxford Street. For a few minutes he stood still on the pavement, watching the people go by, and then, turning to the nearest shop window, studied his dim reflection in the plate glass. He was dressed in a short black jacket, a double-breasted black waistcoat and tight-fitting fawn trousers with heavily stitched bell bottoms. His neck bulged redly over a stiff white polo collar and dicky, his chin kept well in the air by the convolutions of a black stock with white spots and an imitation-gold horseshoe pin. The pointed toes of his black elastic-sided boots shone like polished ebony and a tall, narrow-brimmed bowler sat rakishly, if rather precariously, on top of his large round head. Joss was dressed in his Sunday best and although he could not persuade himself that he was comfortable in it, he was satisfied that it would pass muster with anything he had so far seen on this, his first, visit to the West End.

Hitherto both his work and his pleasures had kept Joss in the east. Bow he knew, and Whitechapel, like the back of his hand. Hackney, Stratford, Stepney and Wapping were neighbouring villages, so to speak, where he was always ready to drink a pint and listen to the local gossip. The Angel, the Tower Bridge, the Mansion House and St. Paul's were the goals of an occasional jaunt. But the West End, with its vice, its riches, its aristocratic manners, to a poor man and a countryman like Joss, as also to many East-Enders who had lived in London all their lives, was something fabulous and frightening, from which, if you ventured a visit, no safe return could be guaranteed.

Meanwhile the beano had gone on. Beer and yet more beer, rough-houses and stand-up fights, the latest public-house ditties—he had a great repertoire of them now—Hetty and the procession of other skivvies and shopgirls who had followed her; it had gone on like that for four years and had become such a regular part of his life that he now regarded it as a necessity. The previous evening, for instance, had been one of unusual dissipation. The customers of a house in Wapping, kept by Alf Summers's brother-in-law, had paid a friendly visit to The Inkerman. There had been songs and jokes and fights—as far as he remembered, he seemed to have been fighting all night, and how he got to bed he could not remember at all. It was not surprising that he still had a white tongue and a bad headache; and a quiet night at home—if home it could be called—would have done him good. But it was his night off and, such was the force of habit, nothing could prevent him from setting out in search of further pleasures. The beano had to go on.

So far, with youth and strength on his side, he had stood the racket of this exacting life well, and although he was now as pale as any Londoner born, he was still an expert chucker-out, as every lout in the Bow Road knew, and he was always ready for more of the beano. But this evening—although he himself was not conscious of them as such—there were signs that his appetite for the beano was a little jaded. The white tongue and the headache could be discounted as temporary annoyances, which would soon pass after a few drinks. What did not pass, however, was a sudden distaste for the pubs and the sirens of the Bow Road that came over him as he set out for his night off; and not only of the Bow Road, but of the whole East End and the City as well. He was tired of working men's beerhouses and gin-palaces, of frolicsome skivvies and bedraggled back-street molls. He wanted something fresh and less sordid, something more exciting, more vicious even; in fact, according to all accounts, what he really wanted was the West End. The more he thought of it, the clearer it became. He had his best clothes on, he had money in his pocket, and there were plenty of green and orange buses. So here he was in the West End. And yet, so potent, so intimidating, was its popular reputation, that for the first few minutes he felt like a novice skater, dreading the ice that might sweep his feet from under him; and he needed the assurance of his reflection in the shop window before he could bring himself to join the gay, human stream—vicious, rich or aristocratic, as the case might be—on the pavement. The plate glass told him he had nothing to be ashamed of, and having inquired the way to Leicester Square—the very symbol and landmark of Joss's West

End—he sauntered off down Charing Cross Road, as gay and as smart as any of them.

Confidence once established, however, the thing that had first call, if he was to enjoy himself, was his headache. There were plenty of palatial pubs to choose from, but the rustic sign of the humbler Waggon and Horses was something familiar in a strange country and took his fancy. The public bar was still half empty and a melancholy-looking, middle-aged potman was standing idle behind the mahogany.

"Pint of beer, please," said Joss.

"Will bitter beer suit you?" asked the potman.

"No, that 'on't," replied Joss hastily. "I want mild beer."

The potman gave him a quizzing look as he drew the beer and passed it across to him. "Are you from silly Suffolk?" he said.

"Why, blast, I am," said Joss, raising his eyebrows, "but how did you know?"

The potman threw Joss's twopence into the till and laughed. "Well," he said, "if I didn't know by the way you talked—a man as comes into a London public and arsts for a pint of beer when he means ale, where else in the world would he come from?"

Joss grinned. "I was right a fool to say so," he replied, "but I forgot where I was, somehow. Why, blast, I know that as well as you do. I'm in the trade myself."

"Oh?" The potman now raised his eyebrows.

"Yes," said Joss, "I'm potman at The Inkerman, just off the Bow Road, if you know the house."

The potman shook his head. "Not my district," he said with a superior air. "Have you ever heard of a little placed called Beccles?"

"That I have," said Joss. "I've never been there, but that's in Suffolk, I know."

"Yes," said the potman, suddenly changing from cockney to Suffolk intonation, "and that's the little owd place I come from, bor."

"Well, there," exclaimed Joss, "if I hain't been in London four years and you're the first Suffolk man I've met! Have one along o'me, bor."

"Well, thanking you kindly, I will," said the potman, drawing himself a half of stout and bitter. "Half o'mother-in-law, that'll be twopence, please. Here's your health. No, there ain't a lot of Suffolk boys up here," he went on thoughtfully, "though, of course, I've been here nearly twenty years and I've met a few more'n you. But I don't pay no regard to that, so far. I'm a Londoner now and Suffolk don't mean nothen to me. Why, I've almost forgot how to talk Suffolk now. Excuse me, I must attend to them ladies in the private bar."

He glided away along the mahogany, flicking his cloth, and Joss bent to his beer, not a little disappointed. He was disappointed because for a moment this Beccles man had given him the vision of a whole hour's comfortable Suffolk talk, and almost the next moment had taken it away again. Suffolk meant nothing to him, he was a Londoner now; he had said as much out of his own mouth, and Joss could hardly believe it. He was even a little shocked.

He knew nothing of the social and economic move-
ments that had made London what it was; he knew nothing of the century-long process that had brought, and
was still bringing, men of the fields like himself to swell
its crowds and turn them, whether they liked it or not,
into men of the streets. The attractions of London he
understood and appreciated; but even after four years
of them—he realized now—he had never taken them seriously as constituting a way of life, a way of life that he
could accept for himself. For him they were like the attractions of some foreign city to the Englishman of the
period abroad, something to be enjoyed, to be exploited,
an endless beano, in short. But he could never surrender
himself to them to the point of calling himself a Londoner, any more than the Englishman abroad would
have consented to naturalization in a foreign state. Like
some of his fellow rustics, but unlike the majority, he
really belonged to the simpler world where he had been
brought up and to the way of life he had learnt there;
he was not adaptable. That was all. There was no particular moral in it, and he certainly had no desire to return to Suffolk, at least for the present; but it was the
first time he had properly thought of the matter and it
was something of a shock to find another Suffolk man
who did not think of it as he did. . . .

The potman had finished with his private bar, but he
was now too busy to renew the conversation, for the
public bar was filling up. Among the fresh customers
. were a private soldier and a woman, who took their
stand at the counter next to Joss. The soldier was in

regulation pill-box and bum-freezer, but the woman was so striking that she immediately drove the Suffolk pot-man, and the whole train of reflections inspired by him, from Joss's mind. She was dressed in a close-fitting gown of pale-mauve silk with frilled sleeves and a train that swept the floor, a fluffy white fur thrown carelessly over her shoulders, a hat with a whole white stuffed bird in it, and black patent-leather boots; and as if to call further attention to these extravagances, she was so tightly laced that her jutting figure, if her hips had not matched it, would have seemed quite top-heavy. But what was most striking to Joss's eye was her face, and in that, not so much her features, which were coarsely and rapaciously aquiline, as the soft, bloomy whiteness of her cheek, which looked, and indeed was, something more than nature. Fascinated, Joss drew a deep breath and, to complete his fascination, inhaled a whiff of per-fume, curiously cloying and curiously disturbing to the sense. At the same moment she turned, and before he could avert his eyes, she had perceived him in the act of staring at her; but she was neither angry nor abashed.

"Good evening," she said with a smile. "Enjoying yourself?"

"Ye-es," stammered Joss, who now had a full view of her lips, no less soft and bloomy than her cheek, her liquid, dilated pupils, and a pile of small black curls under her white stuffed bird.

" 'Ere." The soldier nudged her clumsily with his elbow. " 'Ere's your drink."

He handed her a glass of gin and water, which she

drank off at one draught. Then, while he was addressing himself to his pint of beer, she turned to Joss.

"Where have I seen you before, deary?" she said.

"I don't think you have," said Joss truthfully. "This is the first time I've been up west."

"Oh?" said the woman archly. "Well, I hope it won't be the last."

Joss looked at her and nervously moistened his lips. He could not, all in a moment, accustom himself to the fact that this creature, such worlds above the Bow Road, was treating him as an equal.

"That 'on't be," he said at length, with a show of firmness that did not deceive his beating heart. "What'll you have, miss?"

"Gin and water," she replied quickly, in the manner of one used to being offered drinks, and turned to the soldier, who was looking askance at Joss over his mug. "Old friend of mine," she said in explanation.

The soldier grunted and ordered himself another pint. "One drink the less for me to pay for," he said surlily.

While he was paying for this, the woman turned to Joss and drank off the gin and water he handed her.

"Ah, thank you, dear," she said, surreptitiously squeezing his hand, "that was nice of you. You know, dear," she went on, lowering her voice, "I like you, ever so much. Big, strong men like you are just my sort."

Joss stared at her, tongue-tied. He was no hand at bandying compliments, and in addition, the touch of her fingers had made his heart beat faster than ever.

"Listen, dear," she went on in the same low voice. "If

126

I get rid of that little scruff"—she jerked a side-glance at the soldier—"will you come home with me—you know?" She gently trod on his toe under the counter.

Joss was still at a loss for words, but he could still nod, and he nodded several times, so as to leave her in no doubt.

"Good. Well, drink up your beer," she said, and turned back to the soldier. "I say, deary, you must excuse me a minute. I've got some important business with my friend here. I must be off now. I'll be back later."

She gathered up her skirts and took a first step to the door, but the soldier caught her by the arm.

" 'Ere, not so fast," he said. "Why shouldn't I come too?"

"Oh, it's much too important for that," she protested.

"Oh, is it?" sneered the soldier. "Well, look 'ere, when I've fixed up with a tart, I'm going to bloody well 'ave 'er. D'you 'ear? As for you"—he flicked a thumb at Joss —"I'd advise you to keep aht of my bloody way."

Instead of keeping out of the way, however, Joss stepped up and seized the woman by her other arm.

"Do you leave her alone," he said sternly, in his best Inkerman manner. "She've got the right to go with who she like."

"Oh, 'ave she?" replied the soldier. "Well, what I says is, I 'ad 'er first, and if you wants 'er, you'll 'ave to put me on the floor afore you 'as 'er, yer bastard."

At this point the potman intervened.

"Gentlemen, gentlemen," he appealed, "we can't have

this in here. If you must scrap, please go out in the yard."

Joss looked from the man to the woman, and breathing the smell of her scent again, he felt his cheeks flush. A woman with a scent like that—it stood for everything about her—he had never had such a woman and he wanted her; he was going to have her. He looked back at the soldier, who was, undoubtedly, a little scruff.

"Come out in the yard," he said.

After that things went with a rush. The very next instant, it seemed to Joss, he was out in the yard with the whole of the public bar behind him and the little scruff of a redcoat sparring up. He had hardly got his fists up when the man darted in and caught him square between the eyes; but Joss was used to that sort of thing, and shaking his head as if a fly had bitten him, he advanced on his adversary. The next blow caught him on the nose and tapped his claret; another almost simultaneously closed his right eye. The little scruff was everywhere, darting in for a blow and then out again, buzzing round him like a mosquito; and though once a chance blind thrust of Joss's caught him in the middle of the chest and propelled him bodily half the length of the yard, it was not fatal. He was on his feet in a second, and darting in to close Joss's other eye, after which Joss, far from touching him, hardly even saw him again. The soldier hit him wherever he wanted, with sharp, stinging punch after punch; he had the fight in his hands now. All the same, Joss stood his ground and took his punishment, his fists vainly thrashing the air. The blows no longer hurt him so much, but his arms were flagging; he had to spit to keep the blood out of his mouth and his head was beginning to swim. Just before he lost consciousness, he heard a scornful voice from the crowd behind.

"What the 'ell d'you expect?" it said. " 'E's bantam-weight champion of the bloody Army."

When Joss came to again, he was lying full length on the bricks and somebody was pressing a glass against his lips. Joss tried to look at him but his eyes would not open.

"Who are you?" he lisped; his mouth was too swollen for ordinary speech.

"Don't you worry," said a voice he seemed to know. "That's me, potman of The Waggon. Come on, boy, drink up this brandy."

Joss took the glass—a small pony-glass—from him and recklessly drank it off. It seemed to burn a hole in his gullet, it made him cough and splutter, but it did him good.

"I say, Suffolk," he said when he had got his breath again, "what have become of that 'aire filly with the bird in her hat?"

"Oh, her?" said the potman. "She've gone off with her redcoat. What d'you reckon?"

Joss sighed and slowly hoisted himself on one elbow. "I tell you what, bor," he said slowly. "I shouldn't so much mind that stingy little bastard licking me—and blast, he did lick me—so long as I could have had that filly. I reg'lar fancied her, I did."

" 'Haps you did," said the potman, "but that's better as that is."

"What d'you mean?" said Joss.

"Well, you can think yourself lucky," said the potman. "A bleeding nose is better'n a dose of the pox, I doubt."

Joss sat up with a start. "You don't mean—?" he said.

"I wholly do," said the potman. "I know that fairy all right. I could show you two or three she've sent to hospital."

"Well, blast," exclaimed Joss, "to hospital?"

"Yes, to hospital," repeated the potman irritably, "and that's where you'll end up if you don't larn to behave yourself. Bloody young fool, you, kicking up a row in a respectable bar like that! You ain't in the East End here, let me tell you."

The rebuke went home and Joss was silent.

"And I can't stay about all night arter you," the potman fumed. "I've got my customers to attend to. If I was you, I should stay where you are and have a doss. I'll leave the brandy bottle, and if you're still here turnin'-out time, I'll see if I can find a bit of steak for your eyes, you silly young bastard."

He hurried off to the back door of the pub, and Joss, indifferent now to his fuming, sank back upon the bricks. His head ached far worse than before and his swollen face was very uncomfortable, but for the moment he was indifferent to that. He was trying to think, he was already thinking, of his first sight of The Inkerman four years ago, and of the person who had precipitated his entry there, the man without a nose. This portent had made a great impression on him at the time and he had never forgotten it; but throughout his escapades of the succeeding four years he had never once contemplated the chance that might have turned him into a similar portent himself. He knew, of course, how such a thing happened, but it was a thing that, in his experience, always happened to other people—until this evening, when it had all but happened to him. He saw now with horror what risks, week in week out, he had been taking. His mood and his situation—lying there on the bricks with both his eyes closed up—were ripe for repentance, and, somewhat in the style of Salvation Army testimony, he began to review his past life.

The trouble was that when he reviewed it, he no longer felt really repentant. It was not easy to repent of things he had enjoyed; and he really had enjoyed all those debauches, those rough-houses and stand-up fights at The Inkerman, all those molls, skivvies and shopgirls who had had a bit of fun with him in the Bow Road. He was certainly not "saved" yet. But if he could not repent of the beano, it was at least plain where it was leading him. Not as far as hell, perhaps, but to jail and d.t.'s if he went on fighting and drinking, or worse, if he went on running after the girls, to the pox hospital. And, what was equally plain, he was bound to go on doing all these things, so long as he remained in London. It was something inherent in his conception of town life and his underlying, essential contempt for it. The beano was bound to go on; and now at last, he was in the mood to admit it: the beano was beginning to pall a little. A man could not go on having a good time for ever without a sufficient background of work to make the running, and this potman's job was not work as he understood work; it was too much like having a good time. Work, for him, was work on the land.

This was the real thought—sprung from his earlier conversation with the potman—that was at the back of all his hazy moralizing. Joss was by nature unused to abstract thinking, and now that his thought was out in the open, he went straight to its practical implications. Work on the land, for the likes of him, meant twelve bob a week working for a master, nine or ten hours a day; it meant living in working men's lodgings, or doing for himself in a cottage, if he could find one. How could he be expected to leave The Inkerman for that? He did what he liked there, he was as good as master of the place; they fed him like a fighting cock, his wages were now up to thirty bob, and what with tips and perquisites, he pulled in a good forty-five to fifty bob a week. Already, without stinting himself, he had a hundred and fifty pounds put by. Who would leave all that for twelve bob a week on the land and an empty belly, as likely as not, if work was scarce?

It was now nearly nine o'clock and The Waggon was warming up, as the din from the back door proclaimed. West End pub though it was, they were not above singing a song in its public bar. Joss pricked up his ears. He knew the tune they were singing, and now, the door blowing wide, some of the words floated out into the yard.

Along with those flash girls his money he squandered,
Along with those flash girls he took his delight.

Joss could not help grinning, although it hurt him to grin. He knew now why the young sailor had been cut down in his prime; but he had done moralizing for the present. This was his father's song, and he could never sing it or hear it sung, without thinking of his father in that firelit room at The Rose, putting his hands, handcuffs and all, on the little boy's shoulder and saying—what was that his father had said to him? Something about filling his belly—? Joss half sat up again in the effort to remember, and then it came back to him.

"There ain't only one thing I can tell you. You 'on't never fill him till you grow your own."

That was what his father had said, and with what he now knew of the world, he felt it was true. Only how grow his own? He had a hundred and fifty pounds to spend, and what sort of farm would that buy? Overham Hall, Well Farm, Church Farm, Foxburrows—it would hardly pay a year's rent for any of them. And then quite suddenly the thing came into his head. It would buy Chaffinch's.

Muzzy with thinking, but contented, he reached for the brandy bottle.

FOR YEARS THE OLD HAWTHORN TREE HAD FED THE BIRDS
with its spare, woody fruit and for years had been the
discreet prop of courting couples; but now it was Joss's
enemy, and after a few blows of his axe it was on the
ground. The top, heavy with green haws, he cut off and
tossed on his bonfire heap. The stem he trimmed of twigs
and thorns with his hook and stacked on top of the other
poles; it would come in handy one day for a post. The
stub, however, was not such a simple matter. There were
four tough roots, holding it sideways, which had to be
groped for and cut with the mattock; and when that was
done, the taproot remained, too vertical for a square
blow with the mattock, too loose to stand up to the axe,
and yet too firmly anchored below to yield to the crowbar. Laboriously, chip by chip, he whittled it away, until
suddenly, after holding to the last fibre, it gave, and the
stub rolled over, a lifeless block. Joss picked it up and
felt the thickness of the fang-like roots.

"You bastard," he said, and tossed it over with the
other stubs and roots. There was nothing like a dry
thorn-root to spark and crackle on the hearth in winter-
time.

The blackthorn next to it was even less simple. Its

main stems, the thickness of Joss's wrist, were surrounded by a hedge of spiny suckers, and when he had
hacked his way through them, the main stems themselves were so tough that his hook continually bounced
off them with a hollow clack, as often as not to spike
his thumbs or knuckles on an upturned thorn. Half
severed, they would split and once more send his hook
bouncing off, or even fall forward on his face, showering
him with broken twigs and bits of dirty-black bark. The
only thing to do was to hack away with the hook till
somehow or other you came out on the other side. And
the roots were no better. No mere taproot and a few
fangs here, but a whole square yard of roots, matted together and as tough as the stems. Again the only thing
to do was to hack away, this time with the mattock, till
somehow or other there was no more left to hack.

Joss dashed the sweat from his eyes—it was mid-July—
and looked at his next enemy, an old briar, jagged with
woody thorns. If you got within reach of it, it would
wrap round your legs and seize you by the elbows; if
you hit at its stems, one of the outliers would rise and
hit you in the face. Joss knew all about briars, and looking down at his already torn hands, he decided to use
his chain. At one end of the chain there was an iron ring
and with the help of this he made a slip-noose to go
round the body of the bush. Then he fetched his horse,
which was grazing near by ready harnessed, and hooked
the other end of the chain on its collar.

"Ho there, Smart," he called, "ho, boy!"

135

The horse plunged forward; the chain clicked taut on the creaking stems and brought him to a standstill.

"Goo on, goo on, bor," cried Joss, taking his head. "Goo on, I tell you."

For a few seconds the horse bore on the chain, scrambling ineffectually with its hoofs, and then all at once plunged forward again. The briar was up by its roots.

Joss looked at his watch. It was five o'clock and time to light his daily bonfire; but before he pitched the briar on top of the heap, he paused to lean on his fork and rest. Three days were not enough to break a man in to hard work again, and his muscles ached; but he did not regret what he had done; for it was not just prudent motives or moralizings on the beano in the Waggon yard that had made him do it, that had brought him to Chaffinch's. Between them, it is true, they had put the idea into his head, but once he got back to The Inkerman, the idea itself had taken possession of him, and the sudden desire for the country that resulted from it had been so strong that all other considerations were forgotten. It had not been a mere sentimental urban desire for country pleasures, such as might have been satisfied by an excursion to Richmond Park or Epping Forest; but a desire, a craving rather, for direct and continuous physical contact with the country that, until he came to London, had imbued his whole life; and once acknowledged, it had turned the Bow Road and The Inkerman, beano or no beano, into an intolerable prison. There had been only one thing to do, and in spite of the aggrieved protests of the Summers family, he had done it. Indeed, now he was here, with the clean air and the quiet of this unkempt field, and, more than anything, the sensuous feel of it, all around him, it was hard to believe that he had been four years absent from his proper place.

But there was work to do. Joss lifted his fork and was about to transfix the uprooted briar, when he was aware of a step on the soft turf behind him. He turned round and gave a start of surprise.

"Why, hullo, Edgar," he said.

Edgar was equally surprised, but he immediately recovered himself. "Hullo,—Elvin," he said coldly.

The sound of his surname struck harshly on Joss's ears. He disliked Edgar no less—he had no wish to see him—but he still disliked him as his sometime mate, his sometime fellow labourer. Edgar, on the other hand, as the one word, "Elvin," showed, was speaking as an employer of labour, as master to man, as superior to inferior; and, instantly conscious of it, Joss felt a bristle of resentment, like pins and needles, pass across his body.

"Who are you working for?" continued Edgar.

"Myself," said Joss bluntly.

"What d'you mean, 'myself'?" demanded Edgar. "I heared somebody had bought Chaffinch's and I want the man as have bought that."

Joss stuck his fork in the ground and squared his arms on it. "Well, I'm the man," he said.

Edgar gasped. He opened his mouth and shut it again several times. Indeed, he was so taken aback that, inadvertently, he blurted out what he thought.

137

"Why, blast," he said, "I never reckoned they'd let that go to a labourer."

At this Joss, too, was taken aback, but at the same time it seemed so funny that he broke into a momentary grin. Edgar, meanwhile, had quickly taken hold of himself.

"See here, Elvin," he said, "I've been thinking of making the Guardians an offer for Chaffinch's myself—for some time, I have. Being as that stand next to Ditch Wood and handy to the farm—that'd sort of round the property off like."

He paused, as if expecting Joss to show some sign of comprehension or sympathy, but Joss stared at him without expression.

"Well, then," continued Edgar, "I heared somebody had bought the place—mind, I didn't know that was you, Elvin—and I ran up at once to see if I could do a deal. I don't know what you give for that—that warn't a master lot, I reckon; but I'll give you ten quid over and above. How's that, Elvin?"

Joss shook his head. "I don't want to sell," he said.

"Well, but—look here," said Edgar, "I'll make that twelve."

Joss shook his head.

"But—see here, Elvin," protested Edgar, plainly nettled, "I tell you, I wholly want that. I'm making that worth your while, ain't I?"

"No, you ain't," said Joss shortly. "I want that myself."

"But what are you going to do with that?" demanded Edgar.

"Farm that," replied Joss. "What d'you reckon?"

Edgar laughed. "Farm Chaffinch's, eh? That's a good 'un, that is. You're a bigger fool that I took you for, Elvin."

" 'Haps I am," said Joss, beginning to lost patience, "—but that's my bloody business."

Edgar's face hardened with anger, but he made one more attempt at persuasion.

"That'll be twelve quid in pocket," he said, "and nothen to do for that. You'll be sorry one day you didn't take that."

Joss stared at him stolidly and said nothing.

"I tell you, you'll be sorry," repeated Edgar, and then, as Joss still continued to stare stolidly and say nothing, he shrugged his shoulders and strode off among the bushes.

Joss watched him disappear and turned thoughtfully to his heap again. He was still bristling all over with resentment and thinking of the things he might have said, and now wished he had said; but it seemed so strange that Edgar should want his wretched bit of property as soon as he had bought it, in fact, it was so strange meeting Edgar at all, that he felt quite flustered—he could make nothing of it. Meanwhile he prodded his heap into shape, primed it with a few wisps of straw, and putting a match to them, he watched the flames curl up through the whimpering boughs. That was something he understood. The fire would burn till only a heap of wood-ash was left. The thorns, brambles and briars would be out of the way and wood-ash was good for the land. It did him good to watch the fire; it restored his peace of mind. . . .

The wheels of a trap rolled by in the road below and then came to a stop; but Joss was so absorbed in his fire that he paid no attention. In consequence he was once more taken by surprise when Tod Jordan stumped up behind him on his wooden leg.

"Why, blast," he exclaimed, as he swung round, "you wholly made me jump."

"Well, a nice one you are," said Tod reproachfully. "Stay away for four year, and then slip back without so much as a how-d'ye-do."

Joss laughed. "I know," he said.

"But I've catched you all the same," continued Tod. "I knowed I should. I heared from Joe Kerridge yesterday you'd been seen in Brettsleigh, a-coming down the steps of the Guardians' office; and then as I driv past here, I heared your hook up in the field and then later on I seed the smoke. 'That's young Joss,' I say to myself, 'I'll lay a crown. Only a thick-hidded gret bullcalf such as him'd be fool enow to try and make a do of Chaffinch's.' And I warn't far wrong neither."

He slapped his thigh and they both laughed.

"But what's the game, bor," he continued. "Is that the peelers you're afraid of?"

"What d'you mean?" said Joss.

"Well, all this slipping in like a thief, and not a word to nobody."

"No," said Joss, "that was like this here. I wanted Chaffinch's—that was all I could afford—but I reckoned

if I came along here first and arst about that in Overham, that might put things in folks's hids and some bastard or other bid agin me. So I went straight to the
Guardians—I didn't even look at the place—and offered
'em fifty quid. I tell you, they were that pleased, the
clurk stood me a drink. 'We're glad to have that off our
hands,' he said. But I wouldn't come near till I'd got the
paper business all signed and sealed—and I was right."

"How d'you mean?" said Tod.

Joss raked a few stray branches into the settling bonfire. "You see," he said, "you ain't the first visitor I've
had to-day. Why, that ain't hardly quarter of an hour
since Edgar, young Edgar Clary, was here, a-standing
just where you're a-standing now."

Tod made a grimace. "What, that cocky young sod?"
he said. "What should he want here?"

"He wanted to buy Chaffinch's," said Joss. "He offered me twelve quid over and above what I give—said
he wanted that to round off his property, or suthun."

"Ah, he's allus arter suthun he hain't got," said Tod,
"but that don't fare as if you'd done a deal." He pointed
with a grin to the bonfire, which Joss was still carefully
tending with his fork.

"What 'you reckon?" said Joss. "But what's all this
about rounding off his property?"

"Oh, that!" said Tod, and spat scornfully in the fire.
"Why, didn't you know Walter Clary was dead—these
two years now—and Miss' Clary, his wife, gone to live
with a sister in Ips'ich? So Master Edgar's in charge at

Foxburrows now. You'd reckon that was the bloody squire and his lady, he's that proud."

"He's married then?" said Joss, looking up sharply.

"Yes," said Tod, "but not to Susy Rickards. He soon jacked up along o' her. He married owd Peck the miller's daughter from Brettsleigh. Brought him a nice bit of brass too, she did."

"What became of Susy?" said Joss, busy with his embers again.

"Miss' Clary dismissed her," said Joss, "or so we heared —that was two or three months arter you went off to the smoke—but I reckon that was just that Master Edgar had had enow o' courting."

"Oh?" said Joss, "and where did she go then?"

"I believe she went back to Fleckenham, where she come from," said Tod. "But the last I heared of her, she was in sarvice at some farm or other, I don't remember where." He half closed an eye and cocked it at Joss. "You were sweet on her yourself once, warn't you?"

Joss nodded. "That was years ago," he said. "She might be dead and buried now for all I care."

It was odd, nevertheless, how at the mention of her name, and more still at the news that she had not married Edgar after all, something in him was stirred, something made his heart beat so that he felt it. He fiddled nervously with his fork and cleared his throat.

"That was years ago," he repeated.

Tod tactfully changed the subject. "What d'you reckon you're a-doing of here?" he said.

Joss looked round, his face brightening. This was something more in his line.

"I'm going to farm that—one day," he said.

Tod twitched his mouth sideways. "Tidy job you've got," he said.

"Yes, I know," said Joss, turning round and settling himself comfortably on his fork, "but that's like this here, Tod. I reckon I can do that. I'm going to get all the bushes up first, like you see here. Then I'm going to pare and burn. Some of that I shall leave to grass, but I reckon to be at plough next winter. You see, when I'd paid for the place and bought a few tools and things for the house, I'd still got a bit in hand. I reckon that 'll be enow to keep me for a time, till I get a start, and 'haps buy me a cow and a couple of pigs to root among the bushes. And then, you see, Tod, I got an owd hoss and trap as well, so's I could do a chance bit of carting now and then, market-days. I don't mind doing a day's work for anybody, come to that. That all help."

"Come to that," said Tod, "I can allus give you a week's work in the woods along o' me. Don't you forget that."

"That I 'on't," said Joss. "That'll come in handy, I doubt, when I want a little ready money. That's why I say to myself, 'I must have a hoss and trap.' I've worked that all out."

"Well, I don't know, bor." Tod looked round critically at the wilderness of thorns. "That'll be a damned hard job, and no mistake; but if anybody can do the job, you're the man, I reckon. That's only the thick 'uns as can stand up to a place like this." He took out his watch and looked at it. "Here, bor, that's near on six o'clock. Come along to The Rose, and have a wet. I've got the trap waiting outside."

Joss shook his head. "Can't be done, bor," he said. "I hain't finished my day's work."

"Day's work?" repeated Tod, and then snorted. "Why, you were up at five o'clock this morning, I'll lay, and here you've been at work till near six in the evening. If that ain't good enow for a day's work, I don't know what a day's work is."

"Yes, that's right," said Joss, "but you see, Tod, that ain't only the field. There's the garden too, and the house —you know what they're like."

"But blast me," cried Tod, bringing his stick down on his wooden leg, "a day's work's a day's work, and I hain't seen you for four year."

"Yes, I know," said Joss doggedly, "but that's like this here. If I'm to be at plough by winter, I shall need all my days up here. And if I'm to have the garden ready to plant a bit of green stuff for next spring, I shall want all my evenings down there; and if I don't do a bit in the house a-stopping up holes when I'm done gardening, I shall have a wet shirt afore Christmas. I've got that all worked out, I tell you."

"So I see," said Tod, sarcastically, and his face set. "But I'm thirsty, I am."

He stumped off, dot and carry one, in the direction

of the house, but after a few yards stopped and turned round.

"I say, Joss," he shouted, "all work and no play make Jack a dull boy."

Joss laughed. He had had enough play to last him for a long time, and he bent to his fire again.

JOSS LIT HIS CLAY PIPE AND SETTLED HIMSELF AGAINST the garden gate for ten minutes—ten minutes to digest his dinner of stewed rabbit and admire his button sprouts. They looked well and he was proud of them; for, considering the time of year when he had started, who would have expected button sprouts at all, and in such a garden?

It had been quick-time gardening. As soon as he arrived, he had marked that piece out for sprouts and then, first thing, had cut a faggot—to think of it, a whole faggot of elm-suckers—before he could start digging; but in less than a week he had got his plants in, and now they stood nearly three foot high. Beyond them stood the spring broccoli, almost as high, and beyond them again a bed of spring cabbage, just set out and grown in the same garden from his own sowing. In addition the whole plot had yielded several more faggots, a pile of sycamore and elder poles for cutting into logs, and a large sack of wood-ash, in the process of clearing. The rank laurels were uprooted and the giant box hedge along the central path had been reduced to its proper dwarf proportions. From the garden gate to the front door you could see the whole way, and what you saw was a garden.

This was the first-fruits of Joss's evenings; but the house, too, bore witness to his labours. A new thatch was at present out of the question, but the old one was now clear of creepers, and the holes in it roughly patched, as well as a stack-thatcher could patch them; and two bright new chimneypots stood up straight on the old brown chimney-stack. Down below there was glass in all the windows, the door was on its hinges again, and the light no longer came in through holes in the walls. The patches of new thatch and plaster gave the place a piebald appearance and it badly wanted a coat of colour-wash; but anyhow it kept the weather out; it was a house once more.

Inside the house—well, less said the better; but winter, with the longer nights, would see to that. Before then, however, before the evenings became too short, he must get the rest of the garden cleared, ready for onions and potatoes next spring; he must get a few broad beans in as well, before it was too cold. He could see his way ahead now, not only the next stage, but the next and the next after that, all spread out before him. He could see it so well that at times it was not easy to be patient, so anxious was he to push on. Up in the fields, for instance, he had finished off the bushes and was now busy with paring and burning, which would take him another month or two yet; but even after that there would be some weeks of drain-digging before the day, lighthouse of all his plans, when he would plough his first furrow, and he could hardly wait for it. Meanwhile it was time to get on with the paring and burning.

He knocked the ashes out of his pipe and looked round over his gate. He could hear horse's hoofs along the road, some one coming back from Brettsleigh market, no doubt; and that reminded him. It had been one of his plans to drive in to market himself now and then, to see if he could earn a shilling; but it was the one plan he had so far not put into practice. For the last three months he had done nothing but pay out, he could do with the money; and now he thought of it, the man on the road, whoever he was, might be able to tell him something about the market, and what the chances of earning a shilling were. It was worth while waiting, just in case.

He had to wait several minutes, but when at last a horse and trap, preceded by an ambling cow and followed by a small pony tethered to the tailboard, came in sight, the reason for its slowness was evident. The driver of the trap, a white-bearded old man in a Derby-tweed "frock," looked like a farmer, and Joss was on the point of hailing him, when he drew in to the side of the road and pulled up by the gate.

"This Chaffinch's?" he said.

"That's right," said Joss.

"Name of Elvin?"

"That's right," said Joss again.

"Good," said the old man, "you're just the feller I'm looking for. I'll tell you how that is. I bought these two at Brettsleigh this morning and I reckoned I could get 'em home to Ashbeck afore milking-time. But owd cow's too slow—she's heavy in calf. Well, then, who should I meet on the road but Tod Jordan, the woodman, and I say to him, 'Can you drive these two to Ashbeck for me, Tod?' And he say, 'No, I've got to see arter a man at Brettsleigh as want some poles. But if you go on a mile,' he say, 'you'll come to a little owd offhand farm called Chaffinch's, and there's a bloke there called Joss Elvin with a hoss and cart. He'll drive 'em for you.' "

Joss chuckled to himself. He had not seen Tod since that day by the bonfire, three months ago; he had even begun to think Tod was offended.

"How far is that?" he asked.

"That's near on ten mile," said the farmer. "You go straight across Ashbeck crossroads and arst for Henry's Hall—Ned Gibbons the name." He reached back and untied the pony's halter from his tailboard. "I'll give you a crown for your trouble. How' that do?"

Joss nodded and stepped to the pony's head. "That'll do," he said.

"Go easy with the owd cow," said the farmer, shaking the reins on his horse's neck. "She's a bit far gone, I doubt. Well, I've got ten cows to milk, can't stop. Fare you well."

He bowled off down the lane at a fast trot, and ten minutes later Joss, at a very different pace, was following in his tracks with "the owd cow" in front of him. He gazed kindly on her swollen flanks as he lolled on the seat of his high dogcart and lit another pipe. It was certainly something to be a crown in pocket, but what he wanted—he could tell now—was a holiday, a holiday from the dust and smoke of paring and burning; and this job was as good as a holiday.

Observation had always been one of Joss's principal pleasures. The things he was accustomed to observe were familiar things, their variety limited to the changing pattern of the year; but it was largely their familiarity that made them interesting, for the elements of his small world were so closely and intimately related that anything observed in it—and not least the weather—might have an endless chain of repercussions on the observer. Familiarity to Joss was a symbol of continuity and stability, a sign that his world was in its place, and he with it; he was never tired of observing his own familiar things.

It was a fine October day, without a touch of frost, and the leaves had hardly begun to turn colour. Sloes and crab-apples, as ripe as they ever would be, hung from sagging branches. Children were gathering hazelnuts or filling their pockets with the fat acorns and horse chestnuts that littered the lanes. Twittering flocks of tits and finches swept from bush to bush in search of food; a stoat scurried across the road, a rabbit tittuped to cover. Beyond the hedges a covey of partridges burst into flight, a cock pheasant strutted in the stubble. Everywhere men were at plough or muckcart—you could tell by the smell when you could not see—and some were already getting in their winter corn. Smoke from cottage chimneys rose blue and straight against a clear, still sky; a walnut-tree was in course of brushing and the whole air around was spicy with it. The cart jogged and swayed in gentle rhythm with the click of the horse's hoofs and the grating of its wheels on flint and grit. It was four years since Joss had been through such an autumn scene, and he gave himself up to the trance-like pleasure of observing it. He was so happy that he wished the road to Ashbeck might go on for ever.

But the road, like other roads, drew to its end. Ashbeck crossroads was in front of him and he pulled up by a farmyard gate where an elderly man stood watching him.

"Can you tell me the way to Henry's Hall?" he said.

"Yes, second drift on the left," replied the man, who now had his eye on the cow. "I say, bor, do you know that animal o' yourn is now a-going to calve. Hey, get her in quick." He swung open the yard gate. "Get her in afore she lay down."

By dint of some thwacking and prodding they managed to keep her on her legs, and drove her into an empty stable, where she sank down, lowing faintly.

"Good thing she didn't calve on the road," said the man, as they stood by, getting their breath.

"Yes, bor," said Joss, "I'm obliged to you."

"You're welcome," said the man. "These 'll be the things Ned Gibbons bought at Brettsleigh, I doubt?"

"That's right," said Joss. "I'm now a-fetching 'em for him."

"Oh, well then, I'll see arter the owd cow," said the man. "Me and Ned are mates—we help each other. Just you tell him she's along of Albert Stebbings at Judgment Farm. That'll be all right. And you'd better be getting on with that 'aire pony, if you want to be home afore dark."

"Yes," said Joss, "I'll now be a-going."

"But you 'on't be long afore you're back," shouted Albert Stebbings, as Joss moved off, "not if I know Ned Gibbons."

He was quite right, and in less than half an hour Joss came trotting back to the gate with Ned Gibbons on the seat beside him.

"How is she, Albert?" he said, as they both climbed down.

"Hain't done yet," said Albert Stebbings, "but don't you trouble. She's half tidy."

He winked at Joss as Ned Gibbons pushed anxiously by him into the stable.

"I knew the owd codger 'd come," he said. "Sort of man as can't rest if an owd hin's laying an egg. But see here, bor. You can't get home afore dark now, unless you drive suthun shameful. So there's a cup of tea for you in the kitchen. Just you go round to the back door. The housekeeper know." He winked again and dived into the stable after Ned Gibbons.

"Much obliged, I'm sure," said Joss, and having tied his horse and trap to the gate, he clumped round to the back door of the farmhouse. He was hungry now and a nice cup of tea was just the conclusion his afternoon demanded, a nice cup of tea on a nice white tablecloth, with a plate of bread and butter, a home-made currant cake and a cosy fire in the kitchen grate--it would be a change from the bread and treacle of the last three months. In this expectant frame of mind he rapped his knuckles on the door.

"Do you let yourself in," came a woman's voice in answer. "I've got my hands full."

Joss did what he was told; and it was just as he had expected. There was a white tablecloth on the table, there was a plate of bread and butter, there was a currant cake; and bent over a glistening grate, the housekeeper was busy with kettle and teapot.

"Good evening, ma'am," said Joss, as she turned round with the full teapot in her hand.

"Good evening—well, there!" she exclaimed, and her eyes widened, staring at him. "I thought you were up at London."

Joss stared back at her. She was older and plumper, of course, but there was no mistaking that nose.

"That ain't Susy Rickards?" he gasped.

Susy nodded. "But what am I doing?" she said. "Let me pour out your tea."

The tea had not properly drawn, but it was evidently a relief to her to have something to do. It was only a momentary one, however; for her hand was shaking so that she splashed the tea all over his saucer. Conversation, it seemed, was the lesser embarrassment after all.

"What are you doing here?" she asked.

Joss took a deep breath, in the hope that his heart would slow down a little, but it beat even faster.

"I'm at—I'm at Chaffinch's," he stammered.

"Chaffinch's?" she repeated, none the wiser.

"Yes, that little owd place next to Foxburrows," he said. "Over agin Ditch Wood."

"Ditch Wood? Oh, I know." Susy blushed and turned her head away. "What you want to go there for?"

Joss shrugged his shoulders. "I wanted a place of my own," he said.

"Ah, I see." She nodded understandingly.

"What are you doing here?" said Joss, to keep the conversation going.

"Well, I've got to earn my living," she replied. "But just look at me, supposed to be getting your tea, and you a-sitting there with an empty plate!" She gave a nervous giggle and in a moment they were both laughing at each other. They laughed quite immoderately, but it did them good.

"Here, help yourself," she said at last, wiping her eyes and pushing the bread-and-butter plate towards him. "Would you like some plum jam?"

"No, thank you," said Joss with his mouth full, "this bread and butter is right beautiful." The laugh had eased his embarrassment and he remembered he was hungry. "Funny thing," he went on after another mouthful, "funny thing, I half reckoned you'd be still up at Foxburrows when I came back."

Susy made a grimace and shook her head. "Edgar soon gave me the push," she said.

Joss drank half a cupful of tea and smacked his lips. It was hot and refreshing. It cleared his head and he saw no reason why he should not know the truth.

"What made you take up along of Edgar?" he said.

Susy blushed again, but she was no longer afraid to look him in the face. "Well, Joss," she faltered, "I'm—I'm that ashamed to tell you, but well, that warn't nothen but the main chance."

Joss gave her a puzzled look.

"You see," she went on, "I'd allus been so pore—we were ten in family at home—and Edgar, he arst me to walk out reg'lar, and he told his father. I wholly reckoned he was going to marry me."

"Ah, yes, I see," said Joss, slowly and not unsympathetically; he had been poor himself. "But what, what made him—"

"Made him give me the push?" said Susy, helping him out. "Why, I reckon that was the same as made me do that along o' you, Joss. That was the main chance. You see, he got in along o' this Peck the miller's daughter at Brettsleigh, and well, she warn't much to look at, but she'd got a bit of money. So one day Miss' Clary give me a month's wages and tell me to go home. 'You marn't trouble arter Master Edgar no more,' she say. 'Do, I can't give you a good character.'"

"Well, blast!" said Joss, savagely cutting a slice of cake.

"No, no," she interposed, "I reckon I only got what I desarved. Here, let me give you another cup of tea. You seem to like that cake, Joss."

"That's a master good cake," said Joss, watching her fill his cup. "I hain't ate a cake like that for months."

"Well, I made that," said Susy with a satisfied smile,

and sat down opposite him. "Yes," she went on reflectively, "I reckon I got what I desarved. Not but what I was half glad he didn't marry me—I'm sorry for his wife. You see, Joss, I liked you better. Mind you, I ain't arter nothen," she added sharply, "but I liked you better." She lowered her eyes and coloured to the ears. "You know the way I mean, Joss."

Joss nodded and fiddled with his teaspoon. "Do you remember Ditch Wood?" he said. His heart was beating hard again, but something made him say it.

Susy stared at her apron. "I wholly do," she said huskily. "I was that hot, warn't I?"

They were both silent, and then all at once there were steps at the kitchen door. The latch rattled and Susy's master burst excitedly in.

"Hey, Joss," he cried, "that's a heifer calf. Reg'lar little beauty, she is, and Ned want to treat us to a pint down at Ashbeck Swan, so you'll have to shut the chickens up to-night, Susy." He seized Joss by the arm. "Come on, bor," he said. "Owd Ned can't wait, and that 'on't be one pint neither."

The field behind Chaffinch's wore the appearance of some devastated battleground. The uprooting of its bushes had left it scarred all over with minor craters, and most of the intervening space had been pared clean of turf, which was piled at regular intervals in heaps, some of them still green, some feebly smoking, and some already calcined to grey-brown ash. Over all hung the smell of smoke, not rich, honest wood-smoke, but the

dusty, unnatural fumes of something not meant for burning.

In the one remaining green corner Joss was at work
with the spade. A dry autumn had made the soil like
brick and it needed all his strength to skim off the
top two or three inches. But this was the least of his
troubles, for his spade suddenly caught a hidden thorn-
root, missed by his mattock, and jarred his arm to the
elbow. He swore and hurled his spade at the turf again.
This time he struck a large flint and though it did not
jar him, he drew his spade out badly buckled. He swore
once again and threw the tool down in a rage. A new
spade, that was what that meant.

Further down on the slope a vigorous column of white
smoke told him that one of his turf smoulder-fires had
burnt through, and he hurried down to close the gap.
But the heap had already caved in and the fire would
have to be built all over again. Just as he was peering at
it, a vicious gust of wind pounced into the heart of the
fire and enveloped him in a cloud of hot, fine ash, which
half choked and blinded him. Joss swore a third time.
Everything was going wrong this afternoon and he
vented his exasperation on the heap by kicking it to
pieces; but he was not deceived by this childish display
of violence. He knew quite well that it was all his own
fault. His mind was not on his work, and it was really
himself that he was kicking in that heap of turf, himself for being a fool.

Meeting Susy like that—he could not forget it, and
the thought of it continually excited him. He did not

know why it excited him; he had made no attempt to think things out or to review the past in the light of new evidence. It was the present Susy, not the Susy of four years ago, that now occupied his mind, and the two were not quite the same. Time had picked out certain of her features. Her thick lips were thicker, her Grecian nose bolder, and, it seemed, more Grecian; and her large brown eyes had sunk deeper between brow and cheekbone. The sum of these changes was a slight coarsening of outline, but it had given her face character and, with the general plumping out of her body, it had made her more of a woman. In the same period Joss's taste had changed too, and he found her more desirable thus in her new sobriety than four years ago in her girlish playfulness. Indeed, it was like meeting a new woman, with all the attraction of novelty; but her background was the background of Susy, and above all her unabashed frankness—he was glad that had not changed, and it still made his heart beat to think of. She had liked him better than Edgar, she had said.

With all this in mind, however, Joss had hardly formulated any specific desire, let alone a plan, for the future. All he wanted was to be with Susy again as soon as possible, to see her and talk to her, and that was where he had been a fool. He had just let Albert Stebbings drag him off to Ashbeck Swan without a word, without even a good-bye; and now he was ten miles away. He had made no assignation; he did not even know if she wanted to see him again.

By the time he had got his turf fire alight again, it

was tea-time, and he walked down the hill to the cottage. His throat was gritty with ash, he badly needed a cup of tea; but—there would be no white tablecloth, no plate of bread and butter, no currant cake; he did not look forward to it. When he opened the kitchen door, however, there was, not a tablecloth, but a clean sheet of newspaper on the table, and there was a plate of bread and butter. There were also two cups and saucers, two plates and two knives, his sugar basin and milk-jug, all in their proper places; the kettle was singing on the hob with the teapot beside it, set to warm. Joss looked round him, amazed, and then Susy walked in through the backhouse door.

"Well, I never!" he said, but now he had said it, she was not half the surprise that the plate of bread and butter had been. It seemed quite natural that she should be there.

"Hullo, Joss," she said with a smile, as if it seemed equally natural to her. "That was my half-day off and I said I was going home to my sister's at Fleckenham; but I thought I'd pay you a visit instead."

"That ain't right a mucher for visiting," said Joss, with an apologetic glance at his old deal table and pair of Windsor chairs—the present total of his kitchen furniture.

Susy laughed. "Well, I've been toiting up a bit," she said. "I couldn't see you about when I came, so I thought I'd get you a cup of tea. I was now washing up that pile of dirty dishes in the backhouse. But do you sit down and let me make the tea."

Joss sat down and stretched his legs with a grunt of contentment. A nice fire and a cup of tea ready waiting for him—that was what he wanted.

"I'm afraid there ain't only bread and treacle for tea," he said, once more apologetic.

Susy set the teapot to draw and sat down facing him.

"So I see," she said. "You don't live right—right what you'd call comfortable, do you?"

"No, I reckon I don't," he said, looking around him and glumly realizing the meanness of his surroundings, "but well, you see, Susy, that's like this here. I've got to go careful till I've brought the place round like, and bread and treacle and rabbit stew—you can't live much cheaper'n that."

"I doubt not," said Susy, picking up the sugar basin. "You have three lumps, don't you?"

"Yes, but how do you know?" said Joss.

"Why, silly, I poured your tea out yesterday," she said. "D'you think I should forget a thing like that?"

"Ah, I see," said Joss, and sighed comfortably. It was nice to be waited on; it was still nicer to be remembered.

"Becourse," he went on, helping himself to black treacle from the stone jar, "there'll soon be some button sprouts in the garden, and cauliflower next spring. And I don't say but what I couldn't get a few more sticks to make that more comfortable indoors like. But what's the good? I'm allus a-doing till long arter dark; I hain't got the time to set, and I hain't got the time to do house-work."

"Becourse, you hain't," said Susy warmly, "not by yourself, you hain't."

"But I tell you what, Susy," he went on eagerly, only too glad to have found a listener, "once I've got the land broke up, that'll be wholly different."

"Yes, that's right," said Susy. Her eyes were fixed on his and she was not missing a word. She was a good listener.

"And that 'on't be so long neither," he went on, and inadvertently helped himself to another spoonful of treacle. "I've still got a bit of paring and burning to do, and a bit of draining arter that. I reckon I shall be at plough arter Christmas."

"That'll be in good time for harvest," said Susy sagaciously; she had not lived on a farm for nothing.

"Yes, yes," said Joss, "—but how I run on! Help yourself to treacle, Susy." He handed her the spoon and ate a mouthful; but he could not keep off his pet subject for long.

"Yes, I shall be all right arter that," he said. "I shall have time to go out and earn a shilling then. I can do a day's hoeing or throshing, I can cart stuff market-days, I can help Tod Jordan in the woods and sell a few rabbits, you see."

Susy nodded.

"Then chance-time you can make a bit a-walnut-brushing, or at funerals, when they want bearers. That all help."

Susy nodded again. "That wholly do," she said.

"Becourse," continued Joss, "that ain't only to tide

over like. Once the land begin to bear, that'll be different agin. And by then I reckon we ought to have a cow and a pig or two—"

He stopped abruptly. He had not intended it at all, but the thing had happened of itself, the word had slipped out; he had proposed to her. He knew what he had done, and with a pounding heart he watched its effect on her. He saw her gasp and then blush, and then take hold of herself.

"I can milk all right," she said quite coolly.

"Why, blast!" he exclaimed, and stared at her. She had accepted him.

"And I'm used to pigs," she added, smiling.

Joss, now feeling better, smiled too; but though he felt better, he also felt very humble.

"Still, I know," he said, "the way I live—I hain't got the right to arst a gal to live like that."

Susy laid her hand over his mouth. "Don't you talk non-sense," she said. "I was brought up pore and I know how to live pore. Besides, that 'on't allus be pore, will that, Joss?"

"That 'on't," said Joss resolutely. "Only if you want to fill your belly, you must grow your own. That's what I say. But, Susy—" he hesitated and fidgeted with his knife. "D'you reckon, Susy, we might put the banns up next Sunday 'haps—not to spoil a good mind like?"

Susy giggled. "I 'on't say no," she said, "—not to spoil a good mind like."

They both laughed, and suddenly self-conscious, now it was all over, they turned to their teacups for relief;

they were both glad of a good drink. Then Joss began fidgeting with his knife again.

"I say, Susy," he said at last, "are you—well, are you still like you used to be in Ditch Wood?"

Susy blushed and looked down. "When I'm in the mind, I am," she said. "I'm more partic'lar nowadays."

They both took another drink of tea, and then Susy looked quietly up at him.

"Joss," she said, "I'm in the mind now."

OCTOBER HAD COME AGAIN AND JOSS WAS IN HIS LITTLE cartshed, rummaging among the tools. Mattock, axe, spade and crowbar, billhook, slasher and chain, he pulled them out one by one and laid them in the tumbril. They were his bushing tools, all ready for the assault on Ditch Wood Field, and it only remained to back a horse between the shafts. Accordingly he walked over to the stable door, but there he stopped and lit himself a pipe, not so much for want of a smoke—he had already had two pipes since breakfast—as to put off for a few moments the unpleasant necessity of starting out. It was strange how unpleasant this morning that necessity seemed. And yet he was not tired. Indeed, although he had got his harvest in almost single-handed, and had been busy with plough, harrow and muckcart ever since, he had never felt fresher or more vigorous. But he also felt restless, and not at all in the mind for hacking at thorns and briars in Ditch Wood Field. On the other hand, on such a sunny autumn morning as this there would be nothing like a quiet walk round the farm, and he certainly ought to see how things were getting on. The rooks might be after the winter wheat, for instance, or the cows have broken through the hedge into the beet. He did not wait to think of any further calamities to be averted, but strolled out of the farmyard into Clod Field.

Apart from its acre of farmyard and garden, Chaffinch's was divided into five fields, which were strung out between the house and the edge of Ditch Wood. Immediately behind the garden lay Clod Meadow and Clod Field, of three and five acres respectively, the scene of his first essays in reclamation. Behind them lay Fouracre, an arable field that he had but recently cleared, and Tinker's Piece, a little two-acre meadow, once the camping ground of travelling tinkers and still half covered with bushes. Behind them again came the five-acre Ditch Wood Field, so called because Ditch Wood, which also bordered Fouracre and Clod Field, enclosed its extremity on three sides. This field, now due for clearing, was so overgrown that its boundary with the wood could hardly be distinguished any longer, and it was not altogether surprising that Joss hesitated to begin the assault on it.

Of these five fields Clod Field was the apple of Joss's eye. It was the first field he had made, it contained the best land on the farm, and it had just yielded him a good crop of wheat which, mown, tied, carted, and finally flail-threshed by his own hand, now stood sacked up in the barn. He was proud of it, and already the wheat was coming up on Clod Field again. It was bad farming, he knew, to sow the same crop twice running, but as yet there was not enough land for a proper four-course rotation, and he must have wheat. It was bad farming, but the young green blades looked well, and were past the power of any rook to harm them, as he might have known. He dawdled round the field admiring them, making sure there were no bare patches, setting up a scarecrow blown over by the wind; and then, when he could admire them no more, he went on to Fouracre.

This field had been cleared and ploughed too late for spring corn and now carried a crop of cattle-beet, which looked as well as the young wheat in Clod Field. In a month's time it would be ready for lifting and would make useful winter feed for his cows. But that, too, could not be admired for ever, and when a rabbit started up from under his feet, it took all his attention. He watched it scamper through the beet till it vanished in the wood, and then walked slowly to the spot where it had vanished. He jumped down into a ditch waist-deep in brambles, crushed his way through to the other side, and hauled himself up to the foot of a nut-stub. It was as he had thought. There was a burrow, a big burrow riddled with holes, several of them new ones. He had a good look at them all and put his arm down some, to see how big they were.

"Tidy lot of Johns in there," he muttered to himself. "I ought to get a ferret."

As he squatted there, a ray of autumn sunshine struck through the hazel branches and he sat back, letting it play on his cheek and enjoying the warmth. It had often happened like that. Scrabbing in an old rabbit burrow, with his head in the bushes and the smell of bark and dead leaves in his nostrils, and then the sunshine, the leisurely feeling of mastery in his world, of complete happiness. But it did not last long. For even while he still basked in the sunshine, his eye strayed across the further hedge of Fouracre and hit upon the wilderness of Ditch Wood Field. That was where he ought to be, with the horse and tumbril, and here he was, mooning in the sunshine and dreaming of a ferret that he would never have time to use, anyhow.

Obedient to his duty, he struggled across the ditch again and dawdled back by way of Clod Meadow, to make sure there were no holes in the hedge and nothing wrong with the two cows. But the hedge was undamaged, the cows had never looked better; and after he had spent five minutes gathering a pocketful of nuts for Susy, he could think of no pretext for delaying his return to the farmyard. Nevertheless, when he reached the back hedge of his garden, he stopped again to see how his winter greens looked and to gloat over his potato-clamp, bulging with three quarters of a ton of good sound ware inside it; there would be no lack of food this winter, and all the labour he had spent on bringing the plot into early bearing had justified itself. The hedges were neatly trimmed and the house in the middle was bright with a fresh coat of russet-brown wash. The fruit-trees were pruned of suckers, he had planted a row of raspberry canes and a root or two of rhubarb— But at last there was nothing left for him to admire or ruminate on, nothing left to keep him from the deserted tumbril, and he was in the act of lifting his elbows from the hedge—when Susy came out of the backhouse door. She perceived him at once and called to him.

"Hey, Joss," she cried. "I was now looking for you. I've got suthun to show you."

Joss did not need calling twice and Susy was quite taken aback when he clattered into the backhouse.

"I've never known you come so quick," she said, laughing, "but mind how you go. Don't, you'll wake him." She pointed to a wooden cradle where Franky, their three-months-old first-born, lay, and then stepped over to the door of the bush-oven. "Come you here," she said, as she opened the big iron door, "come you here and look."

Joss tiptoed up on his hobnails and peered into the dark belly of the oven. A cloud of stifling air blew in his face, heavy with the smell of wood-smoke and another smell, very different, but quite unmistakable. He peered harder and could just see six dim shapes in the blackness. He looked up at Susy.

"Bread?" he said.

Susy nodded. "Do you wait," she said.

She took a knife and jabbed at one of the loaves. Then, satisfied, she snatched it out of the oven and dropped it hastily on the table.

"That was right hot," she said, sucking a finger. "Just you wait a minute now."

She cut off a big crust from the loaf and buttered it, still steaming, from a dish that stood ready on the table. She cut the crust in two and handed half to Joss, who had been watching her with an awed look.

"There," she said, "that's our own wheat, that is, and the butter's our own cream."

Then, watching each other, they both ate, and uttered no word till the last crumb was swallowed. It was a solemn moment.

"Well, there," said Joss at last, "our own wheat!"

"Yes," said Susy, "we ain't pore folks no more."

Joss grinned. He had been quite unable to express his feelings, but Susy had done it for him.

"I doubt we ain't," he said. "I could eat another slice of that 'aire, gal."

Susy set to butter another slice, and their minds were so completely taken up with bread that a discreet tap at the door made them both jump. They looked at each other with misgiving, resenting the interruption of their rite.

"Knocking at the door at this time of day!" said Susy indignantly. "Do you go, Joss, and send 'em about their business."

Joss opened the door a few inches and stared fiercely out. "Well, blast," he exclaimed, "blast if that ain't Tod! Come along in, bor."

Tod Jordan, in his best market-day velvet "frock" and "pheasant" cords, stepped into the backhouse, sniffing the air about him.

"I reckoned so, I wholly reckoned so," he said mysteriously, and pointed to the new loaf on the table. "You've now been baking, ma'am."

"Yes, I have," said Susy, who had never met Tod before, "but how did you know?"

"Yes," added Joss reproachfully, "and he hain't been near us for more'n a twel'month. So how could he know?"

"Now listen here, you two," said Tod, shaking the crook of his stick at him, "and I'll tell you how that is. First thing I'll tell you, I ain't no tempter of the pore innocent, and if Joss wanted to keep out of temptation, I warn't one to try and stop him. And what with this owd bit of land and just being married like, I 'on't say he hadn't got his hands full.

"Well then," he went on, "this morning I was doing a bit of business along o' Joe Kerridge on the Brettsleigh road—some ship-fells I had from Foxburrows—and I see a tidy lot of smoke a-coming up from behind Ditch Wood, and, 'Where do that come from, Joe?' I say. 'Why, that's Chaffinch's,' he say. 'The owd chimney was smoking like a house afire when I passed. They're roasting a bloody ox, I doubt.' But I knowed different. I knowed young Joss Elvin had just done harvest and had throshed out a tidy bit of wheat—so they told me," he added dryly, " 'cause I hain't been near. I durstn't. And I knowed just how that chimney do smoke when the owd bush-oven's alight. I seed that many a time afore Joss was born; and becourse, I knowed he'd just go a smart young housekeeper. 'Joe,' I say, 'I'll lay a week's beer-money that's young Joss's missis a-baking a batch of bread. And blast,' I say, 'if I don't go down and have a look at that. He can't take no hurt now. He's a married man like.' "

"Here then," said Susy, cutting off the slice she had buttered for Joss, "do you try this."

"Thank you, ma'am," said Tod politely, and took a bite. He chewed it slowly, licked his lips, and looked from one to the other. "Blast," he said, "that's master good bread. That's beautiful."

"Well, Joss grew the wheat," said Susy proudly.

"And you baked the bread, missis," said Tod. "You're wholly a farmer's wife now. 'For she could bake and she could brew,'" he hummed, and did a few dance-steps with his wooden leg.

"Oh, go on, do," said Susy, blushing, and Joss grinned. "A farmer's wife" was a compliment to both.

"Look here, boy," said Tod, suddenly turning serious, "what I really came about—I've got a bit of carting this morning, Overham way, and I could wholly do with a hand, if you ain't too busy."

Joss looked pensively out of the window, which gave him a distant view of the bushes at the top of the slope, in Ditch Wood Field.

"That'd just suit me," he said.

"Will you be back to dinner?" said Susy, more prac-tical-minded.

"I doubt not," said Tod shortly. "That'll be a long job like; but I've got a snap of suthun in the trap out-side. Come on, Joss, we hain't got right a lot of time to spare."

What with being cut off from Tod all these months and not knowing whose fault it was, Joss was still a little shy of his old mate, and it was all the easier for

Tod to hustle him out into the trap before either he or Susy could think of anything to prevent it.

"What is this bit of carting?" said Joss, as they trotted off.

"Oh, I'll tell you when we get into Overham," said Tod casually. "We marn't trouble arter that afore we have to. Nice piece of beet, that."

"That wholly is," said Joss, who was just in the mood for surveying his neighbour's crops, "and see there, Tod, that's a fine lot of mushrooms on the midder."

"That is," said Tod, pulling up his horse, "leastways for October time. I reckon we'll earn a shilling off o' them. Here, take the reins, bor."

He was gone about twenty minutes, and when he came back, he had close on a peck of mushrooms wrapped up in his ample neckerchief. He dropped them in the back of the cart and climbed up beside Joss again. "Look there, bor," he said, opening the "hare" pocket in the skirt of his "frock" and revealing the limp body of a cock pheasant. "Found him in a rabbit-wire," he hissed in Joss's ear. "Your missis can make a Sunday dinner of him."

"Oh, but you marn't give me that, bor," protested Joss.

"Who say I marn't?" said Tod. "I can do what I like with my own, I doubt, and that's now yourn."

Joss laughed and said no more. It was wonderful to be friends with Tod again.

"Now let me see," said Tod, as they came into the outskirts of Overham. "I heared there was a sale to-day at Miss' White's. The owd lady died a few weeks ago and they're getting rid on her stuff. Let's just have a look. We can tie the pony to the fence."

The furniture was all set out in the cottage garden and the auctioneer and his clerk, surrounded by a small local crowd, were doing their business from the kitchen table.

"Now then, lot twenty-six," said the auctioneer, "an elem knife-box, right a good knife-box. What you bid me? Half a crown, two bob, one and six, a bob—well then, some one start me at sixpence."

Tod, who had elbowed his way to the table, trod on his toe.

"Sixpence I'm bid," said the auctioneer. "Come along now. You can't let him go at that."

But they did let it go at that, and the auctioneer turned to Tod.

"What name, please," he said.

"J. Elvin," said Tod.

"But blast, Tod, look here," began Joss.

"Do you keep quiet," said Tod curtly. "This here's my business."

"Now then, lot twenty-seven," continued the auctioneer, "child's wooden chair with hole in seat."

There was a roar of laughter as the auctioneer's man put it on the table.

"Worth a quid to a nursing mother," said the auctioneer, when he had recovered his own composure. "Somebody start me at five bob."

"One shilling," said Tod.

"Well, one shilling I'm bid," said the auctioneer. "The hole alone's worth that."

The chair went to Tod without opposition too, and there was another roar of laughter when once more he gave the name, "J. Elvin." Every one knew Joss had recently become a father.

"You're too big for that, Joss," some one shouted, and Joss, too embarrassed now to protest, went red in the face.

"Lot twenty-eight," said the auctioneer, "a lady's workbox inlaid with mother o' pearl. Right a lovely workbox—just the present for your sweetheart. She'll sew on your trouser-buttons then." He turned round to Tod. " 'Haps the same gen'leman—?"

"Two shillings," said Tod.

He got it for three—"name of Elvin."

"Lot twenty-nine, a fine mahogany writing-desk, secret drawer—keep your love-letters in. Just the thing for a young man. Same gen'leman, 'haps—?"

"Two shillings," said Tod, and got it for three—"name of Elvin."

"Lot thirty, a capital elem leaf-table," said the auctioneer. "Just the thing to put the writing-desk on. No doubt, the same gen'leman—?"

"Half a crown," said Tod, and got it for five—"name of Elvin."

"Lot thirty-one, an iron double bedstead," said the auctioneer, "bear a carthorse. If gen'leman contemplate matrimony, must have a bedstead."

Tod shook his head. "We've got more'n the bloody cart'll hold already.—Give us the ticket," he said to the auctioneer's clerk.

Five minutes later, with knife-box, baby-chair, work-box, writing-desk and elm leaf-table all piled in behind the seat, they drove on through the village.

"What d'you want to buy all that stuff for?" said Joss, a bit aggrieved at being made a laughing-stock.

"Well, nowadays," said Tod, "they tell me every feller get his gal a workbox and every gal get her feller a writing-desk, for when they get married so you're in the fashion."

"But, Tod, bor, you marn't—" began Joss.

"Marn't, my backside!" said Tod. "I know you hain't got right a lot of sticks and I shall get you a wedding present if I want to. Look, here we are at The Rose. I wholly want a wet."

It was now about midday and there were several customers in the taproom of The Rose. Regular farm labourers were now at their dinner, and in the taproom this was the time for the casual worker, and above all the travelling man, the hawker and dealer, the horse-doctor, the drover, the tinker, the tallyman, the farmer on his way home from market—all, in fact, who were in some measure masters of their own time. Public houses, of course, had their official hours, but since by law the "bona fide" traveller was entitled to a drink whenever he wanted it, he kept his own hours, and if the company was good, the whole day was not too long for his drinking. When Joss and Tod entered, an old man, dressed, like Tod, in a brown velvet "frock," with short white beard and shaven upper lip, was holding the floor.

"I tell you what," he was saying, "I've ate early taters in March, I have."

The other drinkers gaped at him. "That was suthun early," said one.

"That was March in Lincolnshire," added the old man.

Nobody laughed and nobody spoke; he had just taken the rise out of them.

"I think I know that cocky owd devil," said Tod to Joss. "That's owd Budge Abram of Gippingham. He buy owd iron and suchlike. Yes, landlord, fetch a quart. No, no"—he grabbed Joss's wrist—"do you put your purse away, bor. I'm paying for this here."

Meanwhile the old man had not yet finished with them, and took a piece of string from his pocket.

"I tell you what," he said again, "if the landlord'll hang a pint mug on this here string from that 'aire hook in the ceiling, I'll cut the string without breaking the mug. There!"

"You'll hold the mug in one hand," suggested some one.

"No, I'll let that swing," said the old man, and without waiting for the landlord, he strung the mug up to the ceiling himself. "Now then," he said, "anybody bet me a pint I don't do that?"

"Here you are," said a young man opposite.

"Some fool as hain't seen that done afore," growled Tod.

"Now do you watch," said the old man.

He tied a loop in the string from which the mug was dangling, took out his knife, and severed the loop; but the knot, of course, held.

"There," he said, "I've cut the string and the mug ain't broke. Simple, ain't that? I'll have a pint, please, landlord, and gen'leman over there 'll pay for that."

"That ain't a bad trick," said Tod to Joss, "only the owd codger's that cocky. He never stop jowing neither."

"Yes," continued the old man, "I tell you what, I've done that trick with a swarm of bees in the mug, and then took the swarm home in the bosom of my shirt. That's how I allus carry a swarm of bees. They don't never hurt me."

Tod snapped his fingers to attract attention. "I can tell you one better'n that," he said.

"Oh, can you?" said the old man sourly; he did not like being interrupted.

"Yes," said Tod, "I allus carry a swarm of bees in the bosom of my shirt, and one day I took home a swarm from Brettsleigh. A master gret swarm, that was, as big as a half-bushel skip, and I took that off the sign of The Shoulder of Mutton. They must have been arter the meat, or suthun."

There was a titter round the room and the old man glowered at them, scratching his shaven lip; they were tittering at him.

"But that ain't the end," continued Tod. "I was that

used to carrying bees about so, I forgot all about 'em and went to bed with 'em still in my shirt."

The titter was swelling to a laugh, but Tod held up his hand for silence.

"And that ain't the end neither," he said, " 'cause when I woke up in the morning, my shirt was full of honeycomb and I had that for breakfast."

Then the laugher broke loose and the old man rose to his feet.

"If you arst me," he said, "your trade must be telling o' lies."

"Yes, bor," rejoined Tod, "but there's plenty of room for two in that trade."

There was another burst of laughter and the old man strode indignantly out. At the same time, the incubus on conversation being removed, everybody began talking.

"Hullo," said the landlord, coming in with the pint just ordered, "where's Budge?"

"He didn't fare to like the way I talked to him," said Tod. "Here, I'll pay. Do you pour that into our pot."

"Funny thing," said the landlord, as he slipped Tod's twopence into his pocket, "you don't often see two velvet frocks together nowadays. I can remember, some years ago, when everybody as fancied hisself had a velvet frock and pheasant cords for Sundays."

"That's right," said Tod. "I wear my Sunday clo'es all the week, you see."

"Yes, toffs like you," said the landlord, "but that's all cords now, plain cords and sleeved waistcoats, for the likes of us. That's only owd poachers like you as wear a velvet frock nowadays. You can't see what they've got in the skirts."

Tod, with the pheasant in his "hare" pocket, winked at Joss.

"Listen here, together," continued the landlord, "and I'll tell you a story about owd Budge. There used to be another bloke in Gippingham as wore a velvet frock, owd Luke Tickler. He was a gret big strong man, strong as a hoss, he was. Well, one day him and Budge both went to Brettsleigh in their velvet frocks, and Luke, he went straight to The Feathers tap and had a pint. While he was sitting there, some moll or other went and perked herself on his knee.

" 'Ain't you going to treat me, daddy?' she say, and Luke, not being right a civil bloke at the best of times, just gave her a box o' the ears and tipped her on the floor, and walked out. So this here moll go off and tell some of her fancy men how an owd chap in a velvet frock had boxed her ears, and they went to The Feathers to look for him. Well, Luke had done his business and driv off home, but a few minutes arter in come owd Budge and they set about him. They throshed him suthun dreadful, they did, and all along of his velvet frock. He never spoke to Luke agin, when he heared of that."

"Sarve him right," said Tod, "I never heared nobody jow like him. Craze the devil, he would. Now I can tell you a story about Budge, together. He used to live just behind Gippingham Church and he used to cross the churchyard to go home. Well, one day he went home so boozed that he tripped over one of the gravestones and went arse over hid. 'Can't you keep your bloody feet out of the way, bor?' he say, meaning the corpse inside.

"Well then, that so happened his owd woman came out of the door, and when she seed him all boozed up as he was, she reg'lar hollered out at him. 'I'm ashamed of you, Budge,' she say. And owd Budge, he wholly reckoned she was the corpse answering him back, and he was that frit his hat wholly lifted off his hid, and he went down on his knees and started to say his prayers. I've often heared 'em laugh about that in Gippingham."

While Tod was speaking, another dogcart drew up outside the window and a minute or two after Joe Kerridge walked in.

"Why, how now, Joss?" he said. "You're wholly a stranger. I tell you, I hain't heared a good song since you went away. Here, landlord, fill up that quart pot of his. Now look here, together, what about a game of bouls? I tell you what I done. I was now at Little Gazing Hoss-shoes and a bloke came in with a gosling and crazed me to boul for that. Well, I won, and—easy come, easy go—let's boul him off agin. Twopence a boul —that'll make a little beer-money, I reckon. What d'you say, together? Do you go off to the bouling-green, Tod, and get the pins ready. I'll fetch the bird in and take the twopences."

Tod rubbed his hands as the door closed on him.

"That gosling's ours, I reckon," he whispered to Joss,

"and even if that ain't, Joe have had one or two. He'll pay for all the beer we can drink, I doubt. Come on, bor, let's get them pins up."

He picked up their quart pot and they strolled out through the back door to the yard, where the bowling-green, known outside Suffolk as a skittle alley, was situated. There was a rough wooden bench along the back wall of the house for the players to sit on, and by this Tod stopped.

"Have another wet, bor," he said, holding out the quart pot, "afore I put him on his perk. You fare wholly quiet, bor," he added, as Joss grasped the pot.

Joss grinned, and squatting down on the bench, he took a drink of beer. He sighed and stretched himself. "That's—well, that's a long time since I was in company," he said, "but I feel lovely, I do. I tell you what, Tod, I do wholly love company."

"What did I tell you?" said Tod. "All work and no play—"

"Well, I'm now going to play a bit," said Joss. "I ain't no slave to the owd farm."

"That's right," said Tod. "I reckoned you'd now be ready, arter your first harvest like. What I say is, if you work hard, you can enjoy yourself, but you marn't work too hard. Do, you hain't got the time left to enjoy yourself, nit the spirit; and if you're allus enjoying yourself, that ain't no change. You want 'em to balance, like a pair of scales."

"That's just what I say," replied Joss, "and I tell

you, Tod, I feel lovely. But talking of work, Tod, what about that bit of carting?"

Tod pulled down the corners of his mouth and winked.

"That was just a few sticks of furniture," he said, "and a drop of beer as we're taking back to Chaffinch's —and we'll take the beer back inside, I doubt. Drink up, bor."

While Joss was tipping up the quart pot again, Joe Kerridge came out with the gosling under his arm and several other customers behind him, hoping, for their twopences, to win it.

"Lovely order for a song," said Joe Kerridge. "Come on, Joss, bor."

Joss grinned and looked sheepish. It was like being in a pub for the first time again, with his first pint in front of him. He had not sung a song for more than a twelvemonth.

"Let's see how that go," he said, staring at the ground and humming a tune. He cleared his throat and then, in a clear, strong voice, began:

One day as I was strolling by The Royal Albion—

CHAPTER THIRTEEN

July 1903

EDGAR CLARY SMILED TO HIMSELF AS HE DROVE OUT OF
Overham. He had done well over that lot of wheat.
Other farmers, living from hand to mouth, might be
glad to thresh their wheat as soon as it was harvested,
for the sake of ready money; but he knew better. He
had waited nearly twelve months, till July, before thresh-
ing out, and had got half as much again for it. He was
now on his way to Brettsleigh to pay the money into
his bank.

That was the way to farm, and farming was not the
only string to his bow. He went to at least three markets every week and bought anything—horses, cattle,
pigs, sheep, implements, feeding-stuffs—anything that
looked a likely bargain, to sell again at a profit. In fact,
more beasts passed through his hands in a month now
than the farm had carried in a year in his father's time,
and already dealing was a good half of his livelihood.
That was how he liked it. He had no special love for
the travelling to and fro, the bustle and haggling of the
market, the fresh faces and the drinks in fresh pubs.
What he liked was the quick, easy profit, free from
the troubles and delays of cultivation, rearing and fat-
ting, the sort of profit that soon added up to a good

round sum and enabled you to make more profit. He still paid rent for his farm, but it would not be long now before, with the help of his wife's bit of money, he would be able to buy it outright, and then, with the saving in rent, he could afford a subscription to the local hunt. That would be his first real step up in the social scale, and by introducing him to new customers, it would help with his dealing as well.

And then there was the Trust Farm. This was a farm of some two hundred acres in the neighbouring parish of Little Gazing, and as the property of a charity founded by an eighteenth-century bishop, it had once provided the upkeep of a score of almshouses in Brettsleigh. But since then, what with the somnolence of the Charity Commission and a succession of bad tenants, it had gradually declined, until at last no one could be found to pay even a quarter of its original rent. It was fortunate that at this point the Commission had elected a chairman who happened to be a practical farmer, and he had already taken things in hand. Now the buildings were to be repaired, the fields drained, and the thickets cleared, at the Commission's expense, and a new tenant was to be appointed to bring the farm into condition again—at a peppercorn rent for the first three years.

To Edgar, it seemed just the place for him. It was not too far away to be worked in with Foxburrows, and if somebody else paid for the improvements, he could easily make a do of it, at a peppercorn rent. Best of all, it would give him the very room he needed to enlarge his trade as a dealer. There were plenty of times when he could have bought a hundred sheep or a score of bullocks and sold them at a handsome profit, if only he had had somewhere to put them till a customer turned up. But the Trust Farm would change all that, and his chances of getting it were good. He was a local man, who knew the soil and the markets; he was a good farmer, and, what perhaps counted most, one member of the Charity Commission had just taken the shooting in Ditch Wood. Already Edgar considered the Trust Farm as good as his.

His mind was still on this rosy future when three cows in a field caught his eye, and he reined his horse to a walk to have a better look at them. They were half-bred red-polls and in excellent condition. He knew a man who would give him twenty-five pounds apiece for animals like those, and those healthy little first-cross pigs scampering along the hedge were just what another customer of his was in need of. The meadow, too, was a useful bit of grass, just the place to keep a few head of stock on between buying and selling; and of course, he recognized it now. It was Clod Meadow.

Edgar did not often have occasion to drive past Chaffinch's. Foxburrows itself lay on another, more direct, road to Brettsleigh, and it was only because an elm-tree had been struck by lightning the day before and blocked it, that he had taken the longer way round through Overham. Indeed, if he had not been anxious to pay in his money at Brettsleigh, he would have chosen another, still longer road, rather than drive past Chaffinch's. Not that he was so silly as to let it prey on his mind; he had far better things in his life to think about. But the sight of Chaffinch's exasperated him. To begin with, it reminded him that he had been a fool not to buy it himself. He could have had it cheap; it would have fitted in so well with Foxburrows, which it adjoined; and like the Trust Farm, it was a handy place for a dealer. But, what was far more exasperating, it reminded him of Joss, and however much their respective circumstances might alter, he could not think of Joss without thinking of all the things he had against him. Joss stealing his sandwiches, Joss making a fool of him on the elm-tree, Joss outclimbing him on the poplar, Joss getting twopence from Daddy Haines that he might have had himself, Joss making love to Susy in Ditch Wood—these things were all as vivid to him as if they had happened yesterday; and after all that, Joss had done him out of Chaffinch's. Looking at the cows in Clod Meadow and the barley in Clod Field beyond, he could not but admit that Joss had made a good thing of it; but that did not improve matters. Joss had done him out of Chaffinch's. What had made it even worse, Joss was a labourer, and a labourer's place was working for a master. It was bad enough having to pay him twelve shillings a week in wages, but if he could set up on his own as a farmer whenever he liked, what would he be wanting next?

Having recognized Clod Meadow, Edgar gave his horse a touch of the whip, so as to get past the farm as quickly as he could; but just as he came level with the garden gate, two small children raced out across the road and he had to pull his horse up on its haunches. At the same time, and with equal recklessness, a woman came racing after the children, and he looked at her with interest. It must be Susy, of course, and he had not seen Susy face to face for years, not since the day his mother had packed her off from Foxburrows. For the moment all her attention was taken by the children, who had scrambled up a maple in the hedge and were now disappearing among the branches. She shook her fist at them.

"You young varmint!" she cried. "Would you believe that," she went on, addressing Edgar, but still shaking her fist at the children. "Got the baby in the bucket, and just a-going to give the pore mite a ride down the well! And the eldest only just turned five! Would you believe that?" She turned round and faced Edgar. "Oh, that's you," she said limply.

There was a few seconds' silence between them while they both recovered themselves, and Edgar took the opportunity of looking her over, as he had done Clod Meadow. A trim, cobby little woman, plainly ten years older than when he had last seen her, but still smooth-skinned, bright-eyed and firm in the cheek—she just suited his now maturing taste; she even stirred him a little. But she belonged to Joss. Joss had had her first and he had got her back again; though somehow Edgar still felt she was his property. That was another thing he had against Joss.

"That's a long time since I last seed you," he said, for the sake of an opening.

"That wholly is," said Susy, still a little breathless.

"What made you come and live on this little owd speargrass farm?" said Edgar, grinning.

"What's that to you?" said Susy, turning defiant.

"That ain't nothen to me," said Edgar with a careless laugh, "but if ever Joss want to sell, I'll buy that off him."

"Oh, I see," said Susy sarcastically. "Well, he don't want to sell, and if that's a little owd speargrass farm, what do you want that for?"

"Ah, well," said Edgar with a grand air, and it made him feel quite grand to say so, "I farm in a bigger way, you know. I could work him in all right. But you'll never make nothen of Chaffinch's. You'll allus be pore."

" 'Haps we shall," retorted Susy. "But that's ourn, and I'd sooner be pore a-working for my own than be pore a-working for a master—a master like you."

Edgar stared at her and bit his lip angrily. She was no better than her husband, she had got it all pat; and it was not easy to find the words to contradict her. And yet the angrier she made him with her defiance, the more he liked the look of her, her neat shape and her appetizing freshness. Now that Ethel, his wife, was running to fat, and flabby with it, this was just what he fancied; and after all he had had her once. She had been willing enough then, so why not now? It would be a way of getting one back at Joss again. Edgar grinned.

"Becourse," he said, "you needn't allus be so pore. I could show you how to earn a pound or two."

"How d'you mean?" said Susy with a puzzled frown.

"Yes, when Joss is out of the way," said Edgar, and grinned again.

"Oh, I see," said Susy. She put her foot on the iron step at the front of his trap and springing up on it, slapped him in the face.

"There," she said, as she sprang down again, "so you reckoned I was that sort, did you? You may well go red in the face."

She spoke calmly and deliberately, feeling herself in command of the situation.

"I tell you what's the matter with you, Edgar," she went on. "You allus want what somebody else have got —same as an owd jackdaw arter a bit of brass. He will have that, but he don't know what to do when he've got that. You wholly crazed yourself to get me away from Joss when I was single, and then you didn't want me. Now I'm married, you want me agin. We all know you want the Trust Farm and 'll likely get that; and you want our little owd farm as well. I tell you, Edgar, we may allus be pore, but you 'on't never be satisfied."

"I've heared enow of your talk," said Edgar hoarsely, and shook his reins. "I'll pay you out one day, Susy, I will."

"Pay me out?" echoed Susy, as she watched the trap roll away, and burst out laughing. It was she who had paid him out. She had slapped his face, and she felt better for it, so much so that she could no longer go on being angry with Bill and Franky, who were still lurking among the maple branches.

"Come along down, you young rascals," she said

peaceably, "and don't let me catch you touching the babe agin. I hain't got no time to waste on you, together."

She went back into the garden and picked up Deborah, the baby, who was sprawling happily among the harvest cabbages.

"Come on, Deb, my precious," she said. "Let's go and put the beef pudden on."

Just as she was setting off up the garden path, however, there was the sound of hoofs on the road again, and, always curious of anything that passed the house, she strolled back to the gate to look.

"Two more traps on the road," she said, riding the baby on her arm. "We're right busy to-day, Deb."

To her surprise, they both pulled up in front of her, and then, as both the drivers began to clamber down, she saw that one of them was Tod.

" 'Morning, Susy," he said. "Where's the master?"

"He's up in the fields," she said.

"Oh," said Tod. "Well, this gentleman here want to see him."

A short man with grey side-whiskers came forward and said good morning. He wore a square, hard black hat, a square-tailed black coat, drab breeches and loose, soft-leather drab gaiters, all much as any common farmer might have worn on Sunday or market-day; but to-day was neither, and Susy recognized him for a gentleman.

"Good morning, sir," she said, resisting the instinct to bob. She was a farmer's wife now.

"My name's Pilbury," said the stranger politely. "I'm chairman of the Brettsleigh Charity Commission."

"You know," put in Tod, with a significant twitch of the lip, "Trust Farm and all that."

Susy gaped at him. If it had been Edgar, yes, but what had the Trust Farm to do with Joss? Unless—but she could not believe it.

"I hear from our friend Jordan," continued Mr. Pilbury, "that your husband would let me have a look at his farm."

"Why, sartinly," said Susy. "I'll take you straight up to him."

"You needn't trouble," said Tod. "You hain't only got to tell me where he's now working. I know my way about."

"No, no, I'll go myself," said Susy firmly, and with the baby still on her arm she led the way into the farmyard. She was taking no risks; she was doing her best for Joss.

In the middle of the farmyard Tod stopped and pointed to the carefully patched and tarred buildings. "I doubt you remember what this here looked like," he said, "when you last passed by."

"Indeed I do," said Mr. Pilbury. "I remember it so well that all this is quite new to me."

"See them pigsties there?" Tod went on. "Joss built 'em hisself with his own poles and straw. Dry as a bone, they are."

"Yes, yes," said Mr. Pilbury, nodding judicially. "I can see that. That's a fine heap of muck there."

"Yes," said Tod, as they followed Susy out into Clod Field, "and he don't sell that off the place neither."

Mr. Pilbury nodded again. "I should think not," he said, "by the look of this barley." He paused, to pull an ear and crumble it in his fingers. "Good malting sample," he said. "Make some good beer, that. Nice bit of clover, too, coming up below."

"Yes, yes," said Tod, "he wholly watch his rotation, do Joss. But the master bit is—do you remember what all this here field used to be like, sir?"

"I remember very well," said Mr. Pilbury. "I once came to a shoot in Ditch Wood—when Walter Clary was alive—and it seemed to me then as if the wood ran all the way down to the road."

"Well, you might as well say that did," replied Tod, "and now do you just take a look through the fence at Clod Midder."

"I believe Joss is up in Ditch Wood Field," broke in Susy, anxious to hurry them on. But Tod, not to be put off his duty as showman, ignored her.

"Do you just look at that 'aire grass," he said, pulling back a branch to give them a view. "Them cows 'll show what that have done."

Mr. Pilbury looked, nodded, and then walked on after Susy. "Did he have any help?" he said.

"Not a hand's turn," said Tod. "Hardly left the place for a twel'month. Worked day in, day out, and half the night too, he did."

Mr. Pilbury nodded again and they passed on into Fouracre.

"Hullo," he said, stopping and pointing to the side of the ditch, "is that a drainpipe?"

"That wholly is," said Tod. "Joss drained each field afore he ploughed that—bush-drained, mind you. He couldn't afford pipes all over, and blast, he had plenty of bushes. But well, you know we had a tempus yesterday arternoon—can you see any water standing about, sir?"

"No, I can't," said Mr. Pilbury, "and that's a nice piece of wheat he's got on it. But was this field like the other too?"

"That was worse than Clod Field," said Tod, "and Ditch Wood Field was worse than this."

"That's where Joss now is," said Susy hopefully, but Tod silenced her with a finger.

"Just you take a look over the fence," he said, "at Tinker's Piece. That'd pass for the vicarage lawn now, but six year ago that was all over owd bushes. Grand place for courting couples, that was. But Joss scrabbed 'em up, might and main, he did."

Mr. Pilbury peeped over the hedge and nodded. "Handy bit of grass," he said.

"But Ditch Wood Field," continued Tod, as they slowly walked on, "Ditch Wood Field was the master place for bushes. They say the children of Israel were in the wilderness for forty year, but they'd have been in Ditch Wood for ever, I reckon. And now there's as nice a plant of beet a-coming up there as you could wish for, and you'll see Joss a-hoeing 'em, I doubt. He's wholly a thick 'un, you'll see."

193

Susy meanwhile, in despair of ever getting them to Ditch Wood Field, had gone ahead to fetch Joss, and before they were across Fouracre, he came to meet them, hoe in hand.

" 'Morning, sir," he said, touching his cap.

"Good morning, Elvin," said Mr. Pilbury. "I was going to ask you to show me round your farm, but it looks as if Jordan has done so already. Anyhow, I've seen all I want to see."

Tod grinned and Joss looked at them inquiringly.

"I'll come straight to the point, Elvin," Mr. Pilbury went on. "I expect you know all about the Trust Farm. It's in much the same condition as Chaffinch's was when you took it—not quite as bad perhaps—and we're looking for a new tenant. We don't want any tenant, we don't even want just a good farmer. What we want is a man who can put a bad farm to rights, and you're the man to do it."

"But look here, sir—" began Joss.

"Yes, I know what you're going to say," interrupted Mr. Pilbury. "You've got no money behind you. You couldn't pay the 'valeration,' as you call it. I know that, but listen a minute. We—I mean the Charity Commission —we want that farm put to rights and we're prepared to help the man who can do it. We only want a peppercorn rent for the first three years and we're paying for the building repairs, the drainage, and pulling up the thorns."

"But, sir—" began Joss again.

"No, wait a minute," said Mr. Pilbury, holding up his

194

hand. "That isn't all. If the tenant's short of money—
the right tenant, that is—we'll find him in horses and
implements and seed, so that he can get a start, and he
can pay us back later on, when he's made a bit. Now
what have you got to say?"

Joss lowered his eyes and moved his head slowly
round, staring at his wheat. He shifted from one foot
to another and snapped his fingers. He cleared his throat
and flushed to his neckerchief.

"You're wholly kind, sir," he stammered.

"No, Elvin," said Mr. Pilbury, "you mustn't look at
it that way. It's good business for us. That's why we're
making it worth your while."

Joss looked up and met his eyes. "I know," he said,
"but I can't come arter that, all the same."

"Can't?" exclaimed Mr. Pilbury. "But what d'you
mean, what's your reason?"

Joss flushed and stammered again. He was not used to
stating reasons for the things he did and it took him some
time to become articulate.

"Well, that's like this here," he said at last with a
guilty look. "I'm right well off where I am, I reckon.
I've got all I want and I do what I like. I don't want a
bigger farm."

"But, man alive," exclaimed Mr. Pilbury, between
astonishment and exasperation, "don't you want to earn
more money?"

Joss shook his head. "What should I do with that? I've
got a nice bit saved already."

Mr. Pilbury stared at him incredulously. "But—but

haven't you got any ambition?" he said. "Don't you want
to get on in the world?"

Joss shook his head again. "I'm right well off where
I am," he said.

Mr. Pilbury stared at him for another moment or two
and then shrugged his shoulders. "Well, well," he said.
"I was wrong. You're not our man after all. We can't
have a man who doesn't want to get on."

Joss said nothing, but he felt better; it was no longer
his fault, anyhow.

"Well, I haven't any more time to waste, Elvin,"
continued Mr. Pilbury. "I've got to go on and see Mr.
Clary now, I suppose. I'll make it up to you for your
trouble, Jordan. Good day to you all."

The three others stared after him till he passed out of
sight in Clod Field, and then Tod burst out.

"Of all the bloody fools!" he said. "I took three acres
of wood off of him, a-purpose to tell him about you and
Chaffinch's. Are you crazed, Joss?"

Joss laughed. "Do you wait a minute, bor," he said.
"Suppose somebody arst you to leave your owd van and
go and live in a house."

"Yes, yes, we know," said Tod irritably, "but you
don't live in a van, and that ain't me but you."

Joss laughed again. His tongue was loose now and
he could tell Tod all the things it had been impossible
to tell Mr. Pilbury.

"So that may be," he said, "but that come to the same
thing. Now do you listen to me. I reckon I work hard

196

here at Chaffinch's and that give me right a good living, don't 'a?"

Tod nodded.

"Yes," Joss went on, "but I can allus go off for a day with the ferret, can't I? I can allus do a fortnit's work in the woods along o' you. I can drive my owd cart to market. I can go to The Rose and have a game of bouls or sing a song. There ain't nobody to stop me if I want to."

"Yes, yes, we know," countered Tod. "You'd be busier on the Trust Farm, but that's a rare big place. That 'd bring you in a tidy bit of money."

"Yes, that wholly would," added the practical Susy.

"Well, and what if that did?" replied Joss, quite undeterred. "What should I spend the money on? We couldn't spend that on living, 'cause we don't want to live no better'n we do now. We couldn't spend that on clo'es—unless Susy want to prink up in silks and satins—"

"Now I didn't say what I did for that," protested Susy.

"—Nit on beer neither," continued Joss. "You can't drink more'n you can enjoy, and you can't enjoy that if you work too hard. You said so yourself, bor. 'Like a pair of scales,' you said."

"Yes, I know," said Tod a little half-heartedly; he was beginning to weaken under Joss's unexpected battery of argument. "But you could still have your pint of beer, even if you took the Trust Farm."

"'Haps I could," said Joss, "but that wouldn't be along o' the likes of you. That'd be along o' the other masters in the bar parlour. And I should have to wear a collar o' Sundays. I had three or four year of that in London, and quite enow that was. And then Susy 'd have to behave like a lady and do this and do that, and go to church o' Sundays. And then one fine day Master Jordan 'd come round and say, 'I want a hand with some owd ship-fells I've got to take to Gippingham, and on the way back we could have a wet at Ashbeck Swan, 'haps?' And I should say, 'Sorry, Master Jordan, but I've got five acres of oats to drill this arternoon, and the men to pay their week's wages.' And Master Jordan he'd mob me like hunting, wouldn't 'a?'"

This time Tod did not answer, but turned his head aside and fidgeted with his wooden leg. What Joss had said was true, and he knew it. But Susy had not yet said her say.

"You don't only think of yourself, Joss," she said, in a tearful voice. "I don't want nothen for myself, but what about the little owd boys? You might try and better yourself for their sakes."

Joss looked thoughtful; he certainly had forgotten about the boys.

"Well, I don't know," he said. "That's all according. If you want to bring 'em up different, well, that's as may be. We should have to be different too. But if we bring 'em up to live like weselves, I don't see 'em taking no harm. They'll know how to earn their living and they 'on't starve along of us. We've got Chaffinch's and we've got a bit saved. We could allus hire another field or two, if that warn't enow."

198

"Yes, that's right a nice little owd place, Chaffinch's," said Susy, and sighed contentedly. It would have been a pleasure to do Edgar out of the Trust Farm, and no one could say she had stood in Joss's way; but there was no place like Chaffinch's.

"I don't know what you think," said Joss, suddenly turning to Tod, "but that fare getting on for dinner-time."

"My Lor'," exclaimed Susy, "here I am a jowing, and the pudden not yet on! Come along, Deb."

She scurried off down the drift with the baby and Tod grinned.

"I tell you what, Joss," he said. "That might happen I've got some owd ship-fells in the trap arter all. What about a wet at Ashbeck Swan this arternoon?"

THE OLD SAIL-REAPER LURCHED ACROSS THE STUBBLE OF Ditch Wood Field, its comb-like sails rising, tottering and falling in desperate gesticulation, as if every moment was its last. It was an early Canadian model and had cut many harvests on far larger farms before Joss had picked it up at an old-iron dealer's for five pounds and a quart. Contrary to all appearances, and in spite of the protests that issued from every cog and chain, it continued its unsteady progress around the diminishing strip of corn. Joss had taken it to pieces and put it together again many times. He knew every nut and bolt in it; he knew its ways, and after sixteen laborious harvests with the scythe he humoured them gratefully.

Some distance away to one side Tod, with his new lurcher, Captain, at his heel, was stumping about setting up sheaves.

"There ain't much doing in the wood trade," he had said. "I'll see if I can earn a shilling off you this month."

That was what he had said, but they both knew that he had come for the company and nothing more. On the other side and not so far away, Frank and Bill were busy tying the loose sheaves tossed out by the reaper. They went from one sheaf to another at almost a run, without even straightening their backs, and their brown hands flashed in and out over the pale straw, grabbing, tugging, twisting and tucking in. They were plainly tying to race each other, and even the reaper, if they could manage it. That was the way to get through the work, and Joss, pulling up for a breather, watched them with approval; but there was one thing to warn them against.

"Mind and pull your binds tight, together," he shouted. "We don't want no shoves a-choking when we cart."

At the same time as he spoke, there was a flutter at the other end of the corn and something darker broke away from it.

"Hey, hey!" shouted Joss. "Frank, Bill—stop him, turn him back. That' an owd hare."

The boys were too far away to do anything, but Tod's dog was already after it. In the first straight rush he seemed to measure his pace against the hare's, and then, as if he had found it wanting, you could see him put on a deliberate spurt. The hare was not yet in its stride and the dog gained; he got nearer, he was almost on it, and yapping with excitement. At the sound, the hare swerved, and the dog, himself swerving, but a fraction of a second too late, went head first into a shock. That was the finish, for by the time he had picked himself up, the hare was through the hedge and away.

"Pore boy, pore boy!" cried Joss, as Captain trotted back, his tail apologetically drooping.

"That's the one thing wrong with him," shouted Tod. "He allus will yap, the fool. Hey, there he go agin."

This time it was a rabbit that had broken away, and being a quicker starter than the hare, it was already at the top of its pace. But Captain was coming at it short, from the side. Their bodies met, and Captain, brought up in full career, went head over heels; but when he came up, the rabbit was in his mouth.

Joss threw his cap in the air. "Oh, well done, well done!" he cried, as Captain brought the rabbit, squealing with terror, to his master. "I'll allus take my hat off to a dawg as can catch a rabbit. Come you in, together. They're now a-running."

He set the reaper going again and the three others now left their work to draw in close to the corn, with sticks and stones in their hands. But to-day was Captain's day. He streaked this way and that, picking up rabbits. He caught them short, at a yard from the corn. He caught them among the loose sheaves. He caught them when they had a start of seventy yards; and once, grown wiser from losing the hare, he jumped clean over a shock to make sure of his prey.

Joss stopped the reaper and once more threw his cap in the air. "Tod," he shouted, "I'll give you a quid for that dawg."

Tod grinned. "You 'on't have him for five," he shouted back. "Look, there go the boys."

Far away on the other side of the field, they could see Frank and Bill bearing down on a rabbit, as it darted for the hedge. They were all three converging from different directions, and whatever happened, it would be a matter of yards.

"Frank's got him," cried Tod, as the elder boy raised his stick. But at the same moment a well-aimed stone from Bill caught the rabbit on the head and it rolled over kicking.

Tod laughed out loud and walked up to the reaper. "That was a smart 'un," he said to Joss, "and Frank don't like that neither. He's putting up his fists, the young monkey."

"Hey, stop that, together," cried Joss sternly. "Don't, you 'on't go to the fair to-night."

"And you'll lose the John too," shouted Tod, "if you don't look out. He ain't dead yet."

He burst out laughing again. "Do you look, Joss," he said. "They both on 'em reckon that John is theirn, so Bill have got the hind legs and Frank the front."

Joss laughed too and called to his horses.

"That's better'n scrapping," he said. "One more bout and we're done."

The last straws fell and Joss was already packing up the reaper for its journey back to the farmyard, when the boys trudged up, a little shamefaced, but still carrying their rabbit between them.

"That must be a tidy John," said Tod dryly, "if that took two to catch and two to carry him. Look there, together." He pointed to Captain, who was sniffing with a proprietary air at a row of nine dead rabbits laid out by the reaper.

The boys blushed, and on the same impulse they both tossed their rabbit down beside the rest. Joss looked up from the ground, where he had knelt to attach the travelling wheel, and grinned.

"Listen here, together," he said. "Me and Tod 'll finish off this little owd piece of wheat, so be off with you to the roundabouts. And—here, do you wait a minute." He checked them with a finger as they were about to scamper off. "If you like to come into The Rose about half arter eight, you can both have a pint along o' me. You tied that wheat well. Be off with you then."

At this mark of favour their eyes brightened, but they ran off across the stubble without saying a word and raced each other to the drift, where they both started to turn cartwheels.

"Why, blast," said Tod, who was still watching them, "they're like a pair of squirrels, they are. There they go, a-shinning up that owd ash-stub. No, that ain't, that's the maple, but I'd have swore that was the ash-stub a second ago."

Joss laughed. "They swung from one to the other, I doubt," he said. "They're a reg'lar pair of lads for a tree. Folks tell me I was the same when I was a youngster. 'Proper little eel,' they say. But I warn't nothen to them two. Becourse, they're calming down now, but the tricks they used to get up to! D'you remember that time they tried to ride young Deb down the well when she was a babe?"

Tod chuckled and nodded. "Day you said no to Trust Farm," he said.

"They used to take that babe everywhere with 'em," Joss went on, "—they took her right to the top of an

204

owd Eyetalian popple once. And then, when they went to school—! The teacher used to come and mob me and Susy 'cause he couldn't keep 'em in when hounds were about. They just used to arst to leave the room, and you never seed 'em agin that day. 'Well,' I say to the teacher, 'we send 'em to school reg'lar enow. That's for you to keep 'em in.'"

"Yes," said Tod, "I remember one day I came along when you and Susy were at market, and they were getting their teas by theirselves. Bill had the loaf under his arm and wrung off a handful of crust, and Frank stuck his fingers in the jam jar and licked 'em. They didn't want no knife, nit no spoon."

"Yes, I know," said Joss. "Proper little wild animals, they were. I wonder where they got that from."

"Why, father and mother too," said Tod, with a wry face and a wink. "You were both suthun wild yourselves when you were young. But blast, that's what I like to see. They're too good owd boys; they're real spirity and what you call independent. That's what I like to see."

Joss gave a last tug at the spanner and stood up. "That's just what I reckon," he said, "and I tell you, that's why I'm taking 'em to The Rose to-night. Becourse, we know they've been and had a pint there afore on the quiet like, same as I used to do myself, but Susy didn't care for that. 'They ain't owd enow,' she say. Well, now I reckon they are. A boy as work as hard as them harvest-time wholly desarve his pint, and I'm going to treat 'em to-night." He nudged Tod with his elbow and his eyes glistened. "I reckon they'll wholly enjoy theirselves at The Rose, Tod."

"If they take arter their father, they will," said Tod, returning the nudge. "I tell you what, Joss, if we're going to tie that 'aire wheat, I could wholly do with a beaver afore we start." He pulled a bottle out of his coat-skirts and handed it to Joss. "Drink, bor," he said. "That's mostly cold tea, but there's a drop of rum in the bottom to keep that warm."

"Half a minute," said Joss. "I tell you who ought to have the first wet, and that's owd Captain. He've catched all them rabbits and runned all them miles, he's suthun dry, I doubt. We marn't forget Captain. Here, do you pour out for him."

He handed the bottle back to Tod and squatting down on his heels, he made a basin of his two capacious hands.

"Pore boy, pore boy," he said, as Tod tipped up the bottle. "Come and drink, pore boy."

The dog sniffed at his hands and hesitated, shy of being too forward; but at last his thirst was too much for him and he lapped greedily. He was a slender, tawny-coloured dog, with a faint shading of black along his flanks and a small white star on his chest. His hind quarters were slight, and curved like a greyhound's, but his fore part was much sturdier, and when he pricked his ears and hoisted his brushy tail, he looked just like a fox. When he had lapped up all his drink, he sat back on his haunches, licking his chops and regarding them both with a kind, affectionate eye.

"He's now saying thank you," said Tod. "To see him

like that, with his ears back, you wouldn't never say he'd kill a rabbit, would you?"

"No," said Joss. "He's right a beautiful dawg, he is. How is he bred, Tod?"

"Whippet and collier dawg, I should reckon," replied Tod, "though fare as if his mother did a bit of courting along of an owd dawg fox."

"He's a bit too pale for that," said Joss, stroking Captain's head. "I like the feel of his coat. Clean and smooth, and no grease. He can wholly catch a rabbit too."

"Yes," said Tod, and hesitated, reluctant to praise. "Yes, I can't help saying I'm pleased with him. He overrun 'em a bit and he'll larn to turn quicker. But he can wholly catch a John."

"I never seed a dawg run so fast," said Joss. "I tell you what, Tod, there's nothen I like better'n a good course."

"That's right," said Tod, "when you've got a good dawg. I reckon that's our turn with the bottle, Joss."

They squatted back on a couple of loose sheaves and slowly emptied the bottle in alternate swigs. The fierce heat had gone out of the sun and the only sound that broke on the quiet was the rustle of a grasshopper or the wheezy call of a yellowhammer. The tea had cleansed the dust out of their mouths and the rum was warming their gullets. In front of them the rabbits they had caught gave the prospect of several good dinners to come or several quarts of beer, if they chose to do a deal; and the dog who had done most of the catching was there for them to admire. They felt altogether comfortable and sat thus for several minutes, enjoying their comfort.

"Why, blast," said Joss at length, gazing up at the still sky, "by the look of that you wouldn't say we were at war, would you, Tod?"

"No," said Tod, also gazing at the sky, "and that's just over a year now, ain't that? What d'you reckon's a-happening, Joss?"

"Well, I don't rightly know," replied Joss. "I hain't properly what you call follered that. But young Frank, he read the newspaper, and he say that's going on some months longer. Our army have landed somewhere else. They're fighting the Turks as well as the Germans now. That's what he tell us; but that's all afore my time, as you might say."

"Yes," said Tod, "the likes of us don't know nothen of what's a-going on. Becourse, there's a few chaps joined up from the village, we know. But that ain't rightly our business, you might say. That's folks up at London as start these here wars, and who's the better for that, Joss? I never knowed no good come of wars, and I can remember the Boer War, the Zulu War, the Afghan War and the Franky-Prussian. There was allus a lot of noise and several pore owd boys got killed; but trade warn't never so good arter as that was afore, and that was allus harder to earn a shilling."

"That's just what I say," agreed Joss. "Though blast, Tod, here in the country we can allus bake a bit of bread or catch a John. I don't trouble s'long as they'll let us alone, Tod."

Tod grunted. "Yes," he said, "and not come a-meddling—same as this here ninepence-for-fourpence insurance. That wholly craze you."

"That do," said Joss. "That sort of thing may be all right for some folks; but the likes of us can make out—if they'll let us alone. Talking of the war, Tod, the boy Frank say we shall win that all right. We allus do, he say."

But Tod had had enough of the war. He grunted again and sank back on his elbow, chewing a wheat-straw.

"He's right a bright boy," he said after a minute or two.

"Yes, he is," said Joss, settling himself on his elbow too. "Come to that, they're a couple of good owd boys, both on 'em; and they wholly grow. D'you know, Tod, there was one of these here recruiting sergeants in Over-ham the other day, and he come up to Frank and say, 'A chap of your age ought to be in khaki,' and him only seventeen last month."

"Yes, they're wholly a pair of thick 'uns," said Tod drowsily.

The rum was beginning to take effect on him; but Joss found the present subject more intoxicating.

"And I'll tell you another thing, Tod," he went on eagerly. "I reckon this little owd farm is just the place for 'em."

"What d'you mean?" said Tod, stopping a yawn.

"Well, that fare to me this way," said Joss. "They're right good boys to work, like two young colts, they are, and as you say, they're independent like. Well, what I say is, they're too good to work for a master. That's one thing. And if I'd took the Trust Farm, they might easy have growed up proud and lazy. I'm glad I didn't take the Trust Farm."

"Edgar have made a good thing of that," mumbled Tod irrelevantly. "They say he farm a thousand acres now, all told, and he've bought one of these here motor-cars. He threatened to have me up for taking a pheasant of his the other day."

"Yes, and if I had the thousand acres," said Joss, "that'd be me and not him as 'd have you up afore the beak. You wouldn't call that a mucher, I doubt."

"Well, blast," replied Tod irritably, "I never said I wished you had 'em. I'm glad now you didn't take the bloody Trust Farm."

"Oh, I see," said Joss conciliatorily, but still not to be turned from his subject. "But what I mean to say, bor, I reckon Chaffinch's is just right for them boys. As I was saying to Susy the other night when we opened a bottle of stout—if Chaffinch's ain't large enow for us all, we can hire a bit more land, or if one on 'em want to set up on his own, we might get hold of another little owd place like that—being as we've got a pound or two in the stocking. What do you say, Tod?"

There was no answer, and looking round, he saw that Tod was asleep, his head pillowed on his arm. The lurcher, too, was asleep, curled up at his feet, and barking after rabbits in his dreams. For a moment Joss felt a fool, talking to the empty air like that, and then, the rum suddenly taking command, he began to nod.

When he woke again, the air was quite cool and some-body—yes, it was Susy—was shaking him by the shoul-der. "Wake up, together," she cried, "wake up."

Her hair was falling down at the back and she was panting hard; she looked as if she had had a fright.

"What's the matter, gal?" said Joss, blinking first at her and then at the reaper. "The horses hain't run away, have they?"

"No, you fool," she said, "but the boys have."

Joss laughed and scrambled to his feet. "Get along with you, do, gal," he said. "I sent 'em off early a-pur-pose, so's they could go to the fair. I promised to treat 'em at The Rose. We're wholly going to enjoy weselves to-night, Susy."

" 'Haps you are," said Susy impatiently, "but they've runned away, I tell you. They've gone and enlisted."

Joss stared at her, suddenly grave.

"Yes," she went on, "that was just arter tea. The boys had gone off to the fair, so they said, and I was in the garden along o' Deb, a-gathering a few plums for a pie to-morrow, when Joe Kerridge came along in his owd cart. 'Hullo, Susy,' he say, 'your lads are travelling to the fair in style to-day.' 'Oh?' I say. 'Yes,' he say, 'I now met 'em on one of these here motorbikes, Frank behind and Bill in the sidecar. They wholly raised the dust, they did.' 'But whose was that?' I say. 'I couldn't rightly see,' Joe say, 'they were travelling such a stroke; but that was some bloke in uniform—giving 'em a lift, I reckon. They'll be in time for the fair,' he say, and then he driv on."

"Well, there ain't nothen in that," said Tod, who was now on his feet as well. "Why, only the other day one of these sojjers arst me to get up behind—but you don't catch Tod."

"Yes," said Susy, turning to him, "that was just what I said to myself, but well—I knowed there was a recruiting sergeant about, and suthun made me go upstairs and look. I was a good half-hour a-looking, but I found that at last—under the bolster on our bed." She handed Joss a crumpled slip of paper. "Do you read what that say."

Joss held the paper close to his eyes and read the words out aloud, slowly, one by one, as he spelt them.

"Dear father and mother," he read, "we're now joining up. Don't worry. Your loving Frank and Bill."

Then, as if he had not yet taken them in, he read them over once more to himself and his cheeks went pale. Susy, who had been anxiously watching his face for a sign, began to cry.

"There, there," said Tod, patting her shoulder, "they'll soon be sent back, Susy gal. They ain't owd enow."

Joss shook his head. "They 'on't come back," he said. "I know 'em."

He walked over to the reaper and climbed into the seat.

"Come along, together," he said. "I've got my hosses to bait."

EDGAR DREW UP HIS CAR AND LOOKED OVER THE HEDGE AT
Clod Meadow. It was a cool December morning, but
you could still see that the grass was good, three acres
of it—Edgar measured it with his eye and nodded—and
there were Joss's three cows, as usual decent animals,
but no good for the better-class trade to which Edgar
now confined himself. He stretched back in his seat and
lit another cigarette. Joss, after all, was very small beer,
and it was odd now to recall how Joss's limited successes
had once exasperated him. Why, only a few years ago he
would have travelled another ten miles to avoid passing
Chaffinch's, and here he was, deliberately inspecting
Clod Meadow, so to speak, and thinking nothing of it.

This was not because he liked Joss any better or had
forgotten any of the things he had against him—it would
always be a satisfaction to get his own back. The real
change was in his own life, which since those early days
had opened up, had transformed itself. The Trust Farm
had been the turning-point. It had done all he had expected of it, and now he was farming twelve hundred
acres, half of it his own property; his dealing business
covered most of the county. It was all like a game of
cards. You had to learn the knack first; you had to get

to know the pack and your opponent's play, and then, when you got the lead, one trick led to another. That was the thing he liked best of all.

There were other things, of course, that he liked, such as driving a car and dressing for market-day, as it were, all the week, such as wearing a wristwatch and buying his cigarettes in boxes of fifty. These things had all become a regular part of his life and were indispensable. He also liked paying a full subscription to the hunt and owning a pair of expensive sporting guns; he liked being invited to shoots by other big farmers and being treated like a gentleman; he liked being able to apprentice his son, Sid, to a good firm of auctioneers in Norwich and educate his daughter, Irene, at the high school in Brettsleigh, to give his wife a fur coat and refurnish his house, to buy a bottle of whisky or have a woman whenever he felt like it. But he had no enthusiasm for hunting or shooting, for whisky or women, for his house or his family, and although it was pleasant to be treated like a gentleman, he knew he was not a gentleman, and had no interest in being one. No, the one satisfaction that was durable, indeed, the one prop that, unbeknown to him, prevented his life from collapsing in emptiness, was this going on from one trick to another—farming more land, buying more beasts, making more profit; and now, to cap all, they had made him chairman of the local Agricultural Committee, to help the country grow more food. That not only meant that he had become an important person—it might eventually bring him a seat on the magisterial bench—but it also gave him a knowledge of his opponents' cards such as he had never had before; and so long as you kept an eye on the government, there was money to be made out of the war.

Such were the elements of Edgar's new life, and although there was nothing extravagant in his make-up, they seemed so large and momentous to him that little men like Joss—he regarded them as a class now—had become not only insignificant, but even ridiculous, by comparison. That at least was how they appeared to him as he sat back in his car, surveying Clod Meadow and blowing jets of smoke from the corners of his mouth. Their laborious scratchings, their three-acre fields, their dozen or so sacks of wheat, their three-ha'porths of milk, their little bits of this and little bits of that—it no longer exasperated him because it made him laugh. On principle, at least, he still disapproved of the labourer turned farmer, but so long as Joss farmed on this poverty-stricken scale, he was not worth worrying over. Edgar threw away the stub of his cigarette and laughed to himself as he released his brakes. The most ridiculous thing of all was that this morning he had business with Joss.

When, a minute or two later, he stopped his car at the farmyard gate, he could hear some one whistling a tune in the stable and his memory instantly fitted the words to it: "For he was a young sailor cut down in his prime." It was nearly twenty years since he had heard that song, in the days when he had still "used" The Rose, and Joss, he remembered, had so fancied himself as a company singer. But what struck him more than the familiarity of the song was the insistent, almost aggressive, cheerfulness of the whistle. It was unmistakably the whistle of a man who, for the moment anyhow, had forgotten all his troubles.

Edgar got out of his car, and as he walked up the yard, Joss came out of the stable, leading a pair of horses and still whistling in the same cheerful manner. It seemed preposterous that so small a farmer could be so cheerful.

"Hullo, Elvin," he said. "You fare suthun pleased with yourself."

Joss stopped his horses and raised his eyebrows in recognition. "Hullo, Edgar," he said, and Edgar bridled at the presumption; but Joss was incorrigible.

"To tell you the truth, Edgar," he went on, in a burst of confidence, "I am pleased, and no mistake. 'Cause, well, you know how short of beer they've been at The Rose since the war. Week arter week you go down for a wet, and all you find's the owd card in the window with 'No Beer To-day.' That ain't worth the trouble of going out nights. But this morning Tod Jordan came along arter breakfast and said, 'Do you be sure and go down arter tea, 'cause they're having beer in to-day.' That may be only a couple of pints each, but arter a week's dry I reckon we shall enjoy weselves."

Edgar grinned and then laughed outright. It was years since he had drunk a pint of beer, and he could no longer understand how any one could swallow such weak and watery stuff. When he wanted a drink, he had a drop of Scotch; but here was Joss, almost whistling the stable roof off with joy, and all for the sake of two

216

pints of beer that he had not yet drunk. These little speargrass farmers—there was no question about it—were a joke.

"Mind you don't get a-fighting on all that 'aire strong drink," he said, and laughed again.

Joss, seeing his small but longed-for pleasure a laughing-stock, drew himself in and scowled. He might have known better, speaking his mind and giving himself away to Edgar like that.

"If we do," he said truculently, "we 'on't stop for you, bor."

Edgar pursed his lips and changed the subject; it was no good putting Joss's back up.

"I didn't come to talk about that," he said stiffly. "This here's what you might call an official visit. You know I'm chairman of the Agricultural Committee?"

Joss nodded.

"Well," Edgar went on, "you've heared all about these here submarines and that. The gov'ment want us on the land to grow more food. They want us to break up all the land we can."

Joss gave him a guarded look and nodded. "Yes," he said. "I've heared about that. There was a master lot broke up last spring."

"Yes," said Edgar, "but they want still more—every damn' field they can get. So I've got to go round the farms and see what there is. I've just been taking a peek at Clod Meadow."

Joss scratched his chin and looked hard at him.

"That's my best bit of grass," he said.

"Well, we've all got to make sacrifices," said Edgar quickly; he had learnt the value of that phrase. "Why, I've ploughed up every bit of grass I've got on Trust Farm."

" 'Haps you have," said Joss, "but then you've got plenty more. I hain't only got Clod Midder and Tinker's Piece for the three cows, and I can just make out. The truth is, I could do with another midder."

"Then sell one of your cows," rejoined Edgar, "and grow more wheat. The gov'ment want you to grow more wheat, and they're giving a good price. That's more'n thirty-seven bob a coomb toyear, and that warn't eighteen afore the war."

"That's all right as far as that go," said Joss, "but I tell you, Edgar, I've already sowed more wheat'n the place can fairly carry. That ain't good for the land, and I've got to buy things for the animals as I could better grow myself. I like to have suthun of everything, and then one thing helps another. If I grow more wheat, that'll wholly throw me out, and the price—how long will that last?"

Edgar clicked his tongue with impatience. "That's just the trouble," he replied. "You small farmers allus catch that bad. When times change, you hain't got the land to work things in properly and your backs ain't broad enow to tide you over. Why, with wages up to forty bob a week now, you'd be better off as a labour-er'n slaving away on this little owd speargrass farm."

Edgar threw out his chest and laughed. The contrast between himself and the small farmer made him feel how large he really was, and he could afford to be large-hearted. "I tell you what, Joss," he added, "I'd allus be willing to give forty-five bob a week for a man like you."

"Thank you, I'm sure," said Joss with a grunt, "but we hain't come to that yet."

Edgar's face hardened. He had scarcely expected Joss to say anything else, but he no longer felt so large; and Joss had not yet promised to break up Clod Meadow. However, he had another argument up his sleeve.

"By the way, Joss," he said with a sudden show of friendliness, "how are the boys?"

Joss grinned with pleasure. "Doing tidy," he said. "They're now in France, in the trenches."

"Well, there," said Edgar, "I didn't know that."

"Yes," Joss went on proudly, "and Frank have been promoted lance-corporal. He took three German prisoners the other day, he say; and Bill is his second in command like."

"Well, I'm glad to hear that," said Edgar. "They're wholly doing their bit for us."

Joss nodded eagerly. "They wholly are," he said.

Edgar tapped him on the shoulder. "And I reckon that's your turn to do something for them," he said, "—like breaking up an owd piece of grass, for instance."

The pleasure died out of Joss's eyes. He saw now what Edgar had been leading up to.

"And what good would it do 'em," he said, "if they came home and found Clod Midder broke up?"

"Well, that'd be doing your bit as well," said Edgar, parrying.

"So that might," retorted Joss, "but that'd be doing them a bloody bad trick. I 'on't do that, I tell you."

Edgar's eyes kindled a little and then he shrugged his shoulders. "I can't waste no more time on you, Elvin," he said, and began to walk off to his car. "But I tell you, Elvin," he called back over his shoulder, "they may force you."

"I'll wait till they do," replied Joss.

He watched stolidly while Edgar got into his car and started up his engine, and then, as the car slid away, he saw Susy come running out of the backhouse door.

"Joss, Joss!" she cried, waving her arm at him.

"Why, what's the matter, gal?" he said, as she came to a stop in front of his horses. She was all out of breath and there was a distracted look on her face that he had never seen before.

"I couldn't bear to come while he was about," she said, jerking her thumb after Edgar's car. "But do you just read these here."

She held out a couple of printed slips of paper for Joss to take, but he testily pushed her hand away.

"You know I can't read properly without my glasses," he said. "Do you tell me what that say."

"You, you—" she scolded, and raised her hand as if to strike him in the face; but the spasm passed and her hand dropped.

"That's from the War Office," she said weakly. "Frank's killed and Bill's missing, believed killed." She glared at him, as if challenging him to deny it, but Joss's face was blank.

"What the—what do'you mean, gal?" he said.

Susy stamped her foot. "Why, blast, man," she screamed, "that mean they're dead, dead and gone; and that's all your fault. You never did nothen to stop 'em, did you?"

She did not wait for an answer, but turned round and ran for the house, just as if some one was after her.

"Well, that's afore my time," muttered Joss, as he watched the backhouse door close on her.

He still had no coherent picture of what had happened, or what it meant to him. All he had wanted was to be let alone, and "they"—whoever they were who made the war—"they" had not let him alone. There was Edgar pestering him to break up Clod Meadow. There was Susy carrying on like a mad woman; and his boys— what had "they" done to them? The whole world was turned upside down. He could not think and he no longer had the heart to go to plough. He did not know what to do with himself. Then, as he mechanically led his horses back to the stable and unharnessed them, his mind cleared a little and he knew that he must get out into the fields. It was the one thing. He did not know why, and he did not stop to think; but he craved to be out in the fields.

It was still a misty winter's morning when, with a ferret in a sack over his shoulder for the sake of appearances, he set out across Clod Field. It was not possible to see far, and at this season of the year there was not a great deal to see anyhow; but this morning Joss's perceptions seemed sharper than usual. His eyes missed nothing and he everywhere saw things he knew. It was surprising, indeed, how numerous these things were. The short ash-stub, the tall ash-stub, the patch of spindle-tree with the berries still on, the three intertwined elm saplings, the hawthorn with the bunch of mistletoe, the ivy-bank where he had found a dormouse asleep in an old thrush's nest, and the tussock where pink flowers bloomed white; they were small things, but he knew them off by heart and this morning they seemed important, quite as important as his winter wheat, which was coming up alongside. He knew that off by heart too, and noted where it was thick, where it was thin, and where the thistles would sprout in the spring. There was nothing he could afford to miss.

In this manner, passing from one familiar object to another, he crossed Clod Field and Fouracre, where by rights he should already have been at plough. He paused for a minute or two to watch a hawk hovering over Tinker's Piece and to munch a crab-apple from the ditch, yellow and sweet as ever, after a touch of frost; and then pushed through the hedge into Ditch Wood Field. As he did so, a couple of rabbits scuttled out of his winter beans and went to ground at the foot of a little oak-tree. Joss walked up to it and nodded knowingly. He had expected rabbits there and he went to work at once, groping for bolt-holes and stretching his nets across them. Then, standing in the ditch, so as to command his nets, he put the ferret in, paid out line, and waited. He did not have long to wait. The ferret was running clean, without going off on blind alleys, and the rabbits bolted clean too, one, two, three, four of them, one after the other. After that all was quiet, and in two or three minutes the ferret came crawling back.

"Done 'em a treat," said Joss, gratefully scratching its head as he stuffed it back in the sack, "and four beauties, bor."

He pulled out his shut-knife and started to gut them, leaning up against the side of the ditch and taking his time. While he was bent over this task, he saw the lichened oak-bark gleam suddenly green and silver, and looking up, he saw the sun pouncing through a gap in the clouds. The gap widened, and he smiled as he felt the sunshine creep over his face. "They" had certainly not let him alone; there was trouble and pain yet to be faced; but the essential world—here in the sunshine was final proof of it—the world as he knew it still stood firm. His mind began to work again, and already, as he went on with his gutting, he was whistling the chorus of *The Young Sailor*.

Half an hour later, with the rabbits slung on a stick over his shoulder, he opened the backhouse door. It was bake-day and Deb, now sixteen years old and useful in the house, was putting a faggot in the oven. Susy, red-eyed and miserable, was looking on.

"I've brought you a couple of nice rabbits, Susy," said

Joss, unhoisting his burden and laying it on the copper, very calm and very sure of himself.

"Oh, I wondered what you'd been arter," snapped Susy.

"I've been thinking too," he went on, just as calmly, "I wholly wanted them boys to farm Chaffinch's one day, when we're past that."

Susy narrowed her eyes, considering, and then nodded; she understood.

"But there's allus Deb," he went on. "She'll get married one day. She's a good gal."

Susy nodded again. "Where are you off to now?" she demanded, as he moved back to the door.

"I'm now going down to The Rose," he said, as calm as ever. "They've got beer to-day and I reckon a wet 'd do me good."

Susy, suddenly enraged by his very calmness, shook her forefinger at him. "Oh, you!" she scolded. "You don't think of nothen but yourself."

Joss put his hand on the latch and paused. "I was going to bring a drop back for you," he said.

"I didn't mean for myself," said Susy, now on the edge of tears again, "but what about them pore boys a-laying dead out there?"

"I've been thinking about them too," he said gravely, letting the latch go and taking a step back into the room.

Susy stared at him, hostile and incredulous, waiting for proof.

"Yes," Joss went on, "I reckon the boys have wholly

done their bit for us. That's time we did suthun for them. We've all got to make sacrifices." It might have been Edgar, the way he brought it all out.

"Well, what are you going to do?" said Susy.

"I'm going to break up Clod Midder," said Joss.

CHAPTER SIXTEEN

April 1925

FROM THE EMINENCE OF HIS OLD DOGCART TOD JORDAN gazed across Clod Meadow and the close-cut hedges beyond it. It was a Sunday morning in April, not the bright and smiling April of spring, but the bleak and misty April that is the tail of winter; and Joss was most likely to be indoors in front of his kitchen fire. Though you could never tell with these farmers. They might, even on a Sunday morning, be out in the fields, trying to see how much their barley had grown overnight. However, there was no sign of Joss this side of Ditch Wood Field, which was as far as Tod could see, and he was preparing to trot round the bend to the garden gate, when three cows appeared on the road. They were plainly not being driven, for they ambled about from one side of the road to the other, cropping the thin grass on the hedge-banks; and when, a few yards further on, he espied Joss, sitting on a gate with a pipe in his mouth and staring at them, he whistled to himself. Joss was "tenting" his cows, as they said in the neighbourhood.

"How now?" he said, pulling up his horse. "Is that what we've come to?"

"Hullo, Tod," said Joss. "What d'you mean, bor?"

Tod pointed to the three cows. "Why, Joss Elvin out a-tenting on a Sunday morning."

Joss made a grimace. "That wholly is what we've come to," he replied apologetically. "That's the only way I can get 'em a bit of feed this time of year. You've now come past Clod Midder, I doubt?"

"Yes. That don't fare a mucher," said Tod with a sympathetic nod.

"Well," Joss went on, "that was wholly a good midder, that grew good grass—till I broke him up. And then —you know as well as I do—too much wheat and too little muck, that took all the heart out of the land, and now I've put that down to grass agin, that 'on't only grow owd weeds and watergrass. There ain't no feed there and Tinker's Piece is shaved as flat as the kitchen table. I tell you, Tod, I had to bring 'em out on the road."

Tod nodded again and lit his own pipe. "I can't make out how you let Edgar get round you," he said, when it was fairly alight.

Joss tightened his lips on his pipe-stem and reflected. "Well," he said, "you know how that was, bor. Mind you, that warn't all along o' the boys. Becourse, I know different now, but well, he say to me, 'Do you sell a cow and grow more wheat. That's right a good price.' So that was, while that lasted. You remember, Tod?"

"Yes," said Tod, "but still, you might have knowed better, with the gov'ment. They promised to keep prices up, but did you reckon they would?"

"That's just what I said to myself," replied Joss with

an ironical laugh, "but then I said to myself agin, ' 'Haps I'm wrong.' 'Cause, well, Edgar told me he'd broke up the Trust Farm, all the grass he'd got there. Now that was a tidy lot of grass, and a man like Edgar, I reckoned he should know."

"He wholly did," said Tod with a snort. "His lease was up in nineteen twenty and he got out. And the very next year wheat started to go down. He didn't trust the gov'ment neither."

"That's right," agreed Joss glumly.

"Well, we're now in nineteen twenty-five," continued Tod with another snort, "and how much wheat do Edgar Clary, Esquire, J.P., grow now? I do know he've got acres, everlasting of acres, down to sugar-beet. There's a gov'ment subsidy on that."

"Ah, well, he can afford the labour," protested Joss, "and the more acres, the more the profit mount up. But I couldn't only grow an acre or two, and that have got to be hoed twice and chopped out; and I hain't rightly got the time. I don't know why folks 'on't pay a fair price for their bread."

"What did I tell you ten years ago?" said Tod. "Trade's allus worser arter a war'n that was afore. Same as my trade. Folks send their washing to the steam laundry and 'on't buy clo'es-props. They light their fires with fire-lighters and they don't bake at home, so they 'on't buy faggots. And what with hoss-rakes and side-rakes and wire netting, a farmer 'on't look at a wooden rake or a hurdle. I tell you, they 'on't let well alone."

"No, they 'on't," said Joss, "and that's the same along

o' this here tithe. Tithe and wheat allus went together. Wheat was low, tithe was low. Wheat was high, tithe was high. But now wheat's low and tithe's high. They couldn't keep their promise to us, you might say, but they kept that to the Church. I hain't got nothen agin the Church so far, but what have the Church done for me? And I don't know where the money's coming from to pay last year's tithe. That's as much as I can do to keep a-going along o' the cows. Folks come every day for a pint or a quart—they know that's good milk—and that's ready money. But I must have three cows and I hain't got the feed for 'em."

He stared in front of him, slowly puffing at his pipe, and Tod, at a loss for further argument, did the same. They had often ruminated over Joss's grievances thus, but this morning Joss seemed unusually dejected.

"I hain't seen you at The Rose this couple of weeks," said Tod after a minute or two.

"I know," said Joss, looking up guiltily. "I've been out every night a-tenting these here cows, and well, Tod, I'm tired. I ain't only fifty-two, we know, and I've still got my health and strength, but working like this day arter day, and next to nothen in return"—he turned his face away again—"I'm suthun tired, Tod."

Tod looked hard at him, and not without concern. Through all his ups and downs, it was the first time he had heard Joss talk like that.

"But you can work one afore dinner to-day," he said coaxingly. "That's Sunday and I've still got a shilling or two in my pocket. I know that ain't the beer that was afore the war—we used to leave better stuff at the bottom of the barrel—but that'll do you good if you have enow."

Joss looked back at him and laughed. "I know," he said, "and I'd now be coming along; but—I'll tell you what that is, Tod. You know our gal Deb's in sarvice at Ips'ich? Well, since they started them motorbuses to Brettsleigh, she come and see us once a month. That ain't like the owd carrier's-cart days, when a gal was lucky to get home once in six months."

"Ah, yes, yes," said Tod understandingly, "you're now waiting to take her off the bus, I doubt?"

"Yes, but that ain't the only thing," Joss went on. "Do, I should be up there along o' you in two ticks. But that fare she've been and left her owd situation and she's now somewhere in the docks, a-sarving behind the bar in a public." He raised his hand in deprecation. "You marn't think I mind that, so far. I done the same myself when I was up at London, and enjoyed that. But her mother fare to think that's a rough place for a gal of her age—she's just twenty-four, you know—and there's another thing."

He clambered off the gate and leant confidentially against the shaft of Tod's cart.

"I wholly wanted to tell you, Tod. You see, afore Deb went to Ips'ich, she did a bit of courting along o' young Fred Haines—you know, owd Daddy's grandson, work at the Well Farm. She was properly sweet on him. Well, we reckoned we'd say to her, if she like to marry him, they can come and live along of us. Susy have had the rheumatics last year or so and could do with a hand in the house, and if young Fred 'd come in along o' me, I reckon we might grow a few of these here sugar-beet and 'haps keep a few more pigs—well, I reckon we could wholly make a do. What d'you reckon, Tod?"

Tod put his head on one side and then nodded. "I reckon that 'd be just the thing, bor," he said. "With another pair of hands and no more what you might call outgoings, you'd set yourself up agin, and Fred's right a good boy to work. Besides, that 'd be doing yourself good for later on."

"Ah, I'm glad to hear you talk like that," said Joss eagerly; he seemed quite another man now. "That's just what I told Susy. 'We shan't allus be able to farm that,' I say to her." He turned his head and looked up the road in the direction of Brettsleigh. "I can now hear the bus," he said. "Look, here that come."

"Then I'd better be a-moving," said Tod, wheeling his trap round in the road. "Farewell, bor; but you marn't be too tired to-night."

This last remark, however, went unanswered, for Joss had already caught sight of Deb on the step of the bus and was hurrying towards her. So, too, was Susy, down the garden path, and by the time the bus stopped, they were both there to welcome her. She kissed them affectionately, one after the other, and it was only then, as the bus ground on its way and left a tall young man standing modestly behind her, that they realized she was not alone. There was an awkward pause and Deb coloured up.

"This is my young man," she explained shyly. "His name's Einar."

Joss stared hard at him. He was fair and blue-eyed, fairer and bluer-eyed than would have seemed possible, and Einar was not a Suffolk name, to say the least of it.

"Pleased to meet you, Mr. Elvin," he said, smiling and holding out his hand.

Joss stared at him even harder. He looked quite handsome when he smiled; but his voice and his manner of speech were strange, so strange that Joss could only imagine him to belong to some remote part of the "sheers."

"Ain't you going to say how d'ye do?" prompted Susy.

Joss seized the young man's hand and shook it awkwardly; it was as big and leathery as his own. But he could not, for the life of him, get a word out of his mouth.

Deb, half piqued, half alarmed by his silence, frowned a little and took her young man by the arm. She would show them she meant what she said. She would show them he was no ordinary young man, no mere village hobbledehoy.

"Einar come from Norway," she went on. "He's chief officer on his father's ship, and we're engaged. Look at the ring he gave me," she said, holding up her left hand. "They're real diamonds."

Susy peered forward and giggled in her admiration. "Ain't that pretty?" she said. "Don't you reckon so, Father?"

Joss nodded and peered too, but it was Deb herself, and not the ring, that he was looking at. She was a little shorter than Susy, and almost as cobby; she would be a good deal plumper when she was Susy's age. But she had her mother's nose and forehead all of a piece, she had round black eyes like berries and his own high colour. A girl like that, with her neat black coat, her neat little feet and silky ankles, and the touch of powder on her face—he could understand how the young man wanted her. But her nose was more commanding than her mother's, he could see. She wanted her own way, she would be the master; and still the young man wanted her. But she would have her own way.

Deb herself, now more piqued than alarmed, answered his gaze defiantly. She would show him then—standing there not saying a word and staring at her like that, just as if Einar was not there. If Einar was not good enough for him, well, she would show him.

"We're going to get married in a month," she said, "when Einar come back on his next voyage. Einar's going to give up the sea and we're going to live on his father's farm. That's a three-hoss farm, ain't that, Einar?"

Joss, she knew, had never had more than two horses, and that would show him. But Joss—she could not make him out. He still stared at her and said nothing. The only difference was that now all the colour had gone out of his face.

"Ain't you going to wish me luck, Father?" she said desperately.

This time Joss really struggled to speak. He moistened his lips and opened his mouth, but nothing would come and he could not even look her in the face any longer.

Deb clutched Einar's arm tighter and turned to her mother in a pet.

"I do call that mean," she cried. "Here I bring my young man down to see you, and father 'on't say a word, nit take no notice of him. I don't know why I brought you," she said, looking up at Einar with tears in her eyes.

Einar grinned helplessly, as if he could make nothing of it all. "Where is the boozer, Deb?" he said, in an odd mixture of foreign accent and seaman's slang. "Is there a boozer here?"

"Yes, about a mile further on," said Deb, sniffing back her tears, "but what d'you want to know for?"

"Well, let us go and get a bottle or two for dinner," said Einar, laughing. "Dinner is no damn good without—good health!" He raised an imaginary glass to his lips and drained it. "Come along, Deb," he said, putting an arm round her waist.

"That's right," said Susy, with a grateful smile, "but don't be late for dinner, together."

Then, as they whisked off along the road, she folded her arms and turned on Joss.

"That young man's no fool," she said, "but as for you —standing there a-garping and making your daughter cry like that—you ought to be ashamed of yourself."

Joss swallowed and took a deep breath. It was a real pleasure to hear Susy's familiar voice scolding away at him. It seemed to bring him back to life.

"I wholly thought you knowed behaviours," Susy went on.

"So I do, but, well—" He made an ineffectual pass with his hand.

"Well, what?" persisted Susy.

"Well"—he shifted his feet and looked on the ground —"she powder her nose, just like the tarts used to do."

"Non-sense," said Susy shortly. "All the gals do now-adays. Things have moved since your day, and a good thing too. You'll need a better excuse'n that."

"And then, going and marrying a foreigner like that," he went on, shifting his feet and looking over the hedge.

"That's her business," said Susy, "and he's right a nice young man, I'm sure. A gal must follow her fancy."

Joss grunted. "But that's just what you'd expect," he went on, "a-sarving in a public in the docks. You said that was a rough place for a gal yourself."

"Yes, so I—so I did," faltered Susy, and then came to a stop.

Joss looked quickly round at her, but it was now Susy's turn for embarrassment and she could not meet his eyes. Joss suddenly stopped fencing.

"You're quite right," he said. "Young folks must follow their fancy. We did ourselves. But listen here, gal. Do you reckon—d'you reckon he'd come and live along of us if we arst him?"

Susy raised her eyes to his and shook her head. "Not on a little owd speargrass farm like this, silly. Didn't you hear her say his father'd got a three-hoss farm and a ship? She's going up in the world, don't you see?"

"I doubt she is," he said slowly, and then sighed.

"Yes, I know what you're thinking," said Susy. She stepped up and slipped her arm through his. "You're thinking we've got to make out by ourselves."

Joss nodded.

"Well, I'll help you, boy," she said. "I can hoe a row of sugar-beet, I doubt."

Joss laughed. "I reckon we shall make out somehow," he said, "and leastways, we've got a roof to our hids and a piece of ground to grow our own. That 'll keep us, so long as we can keep a-doing."

"That's what I mean," said Susy. "I don't mind working hard, a-working for my own. Besides, times may change."

"That's right," said Joss, and hesitated. "I say, Susy," he went on, "we must wholly wish 'em luck when they come back, 'cause—'cause well, I know behaviours all right."

"I know you do," she said, squeezing his arm and then pushing him away. "But that remind me. Here I am, a-listening to all your talk and my pudden a-boiling dry."

"God's truth," exclaimed Joss, as he watched her go running up the garden path, "I wonder where my cows have got to."

THE DEAD STOCK AT BRETTSLEIGH MARKET WAS THE auctioneer's last responsibility and as it was still early afternoon, Tod Jordan had that part of the market all to himself. There were the usual tools and implements, the usual furniture and household utensils, the usual odd heaps of miscellaneous junk, an epitome of country occupations and ways of living, inviting both appraisal and speculative fancy. At other times Tod would have inspected every lot with the same care and most of them would have drawn from him some appropriate comment; "I wouldn't marry a mawther as used her saucepans like that," was one of his favourites in the dead-stock sale. But this afternoon there were only three lots that he had eyes for. One was a pile of old harness chains; another was a pile of rusty ploughshares, strung together in small bundles; and the third was a pair of broken-down iron ploughs. These three lots he examined from first one direction and then another; he bent down and prodded them with his stick, and then stood back to sum them up with his eye. He turned them over with his hands, testing their weight, and stood back again, to frown hard and make elaborate calculations on his fingers. He was far too busy with all this to notice any

one, and Joss, as he approached along the paved gang-
way, had an uninterrupted view of all his actions.

"Well, blast," he exclaimed, when at last he came up
at Tod's elbow, "you're cutting a fine lot of capers, ain't
you?"

Tod looked up and nodded, but he still went on
frowning and counting on his fingers.

"What d'you reckon you're arter?" said Joss with a
grin.

"Well, now I'll tell you," said Tod, suddenly coming
to the end of his calculations and rubbing his hands. "I'm
now going to bid for them 'aire." He pointed to the
three lots in front of them.

Joss stared at them. "What, them 'aire?" he said. "A
heap of shares and a couple of owd ploughs? You ain't
starting a farm, Tod?"

"No, I ain't," said Tod emphatically, "but I tell you
what, Joss, I am thinking of changing my trade."

"Oh?" said Joss, taking his eyes off the ploughs and
fixing them on Tod.

"Yes," said Tod, "you've often heared me talk of the
way things are in the wood business. That ain't worth
while making rakes and hurdles—nit walking-sticks, for
folks don't walk like they used to. Becourse, I don't say
as I couldn't earn a shilling a-cutting o' poles and peasticks, but that's rough owd work at my age—'cause I'm
owder'n you think for. That's more'n a year or two since
I planted a walnut-tree for my seventieth birthday." He
thumped his stick on the pavement and stuck out his
chin as he said it.

Joss nodded. "That's right, what you say, bor, and besides, cutting poles and peasticks—that ain't proper tradesman's work like making a hurdle. But what d'you reckon to do instead?"

"Well, bor, I'll tell you," replied Tod. "The other day Joe Kerridge—you know, Joe's getting on like me, and he say, what with these here vans and lorries, there ain't nothen in the carting line, nit in hawking and dealing neither, so he've started a fish round. Well, Joe said to me he knowed there was money in owd iron—there's for ever of owd wore-up stuff about the country, he say, and they're reg'lar glad of that to melt up agin for new. He told me suthun about the price and where to get rid on the stuff, and I tell you, I'm thinking of making a gamble. I was now a-reckoning how far I durst bid for them 'aire three lots. Do you blame me, bor?"

He stuck out his chin again, and again Joss nodded. "No, I don't blame you," he said. "A man must get a living how he can nowadays." He gazed at the two derelict ploughs and slowly took out his clay pipe. "And yours ain't the only trade that's messed up," he added.

"Yes, I know," replied Tod sardonically, "but then that's nothen new. You farmers allus were messed up."

Joss could not forbear a grin at the dusty old gibe, but he shook his head as he filled his pipe.

"All the same," he said, "I wholly am this time, and no mistake. I've now been looking for you all over the market. I wanted to tell you." He paused, as if awaiting encouragement, and lit his pipe.

"What's the matter, bor?" said Tod in a changed tone.

239

Joss took a few puffs at his pipe to prepare himself. "That's this here tithe," he said. "You know I hain't paid that for several year now."

"No more have half the county," retorted Tod. "I reckoned you wholly were going to tell me suthun new."

"Yes, we all know that," said Joss impatiently, "but this morning I had a letter from Queen Anne's Bounty or whatever they call that. They're going to have me up in court if I don't pay my arrears." He paused and looked hard at Tod. "What am I to do, bor?"

Tod pushed back his cap and scratched his head. "Well, blast!" he exclaimed.

"You know that ain't for want of working," continued Joss, "nit of growing good stuff; but what's the good of working and growing good stuff if nobody'll give you a fair price?"

"Yes," said Tod thoughtfully, "these are rum times for everybody. Here's almost twelve years since the war ended, and times don't get no better. We don't understand 'em, nit nobody else, I reckon. You have to get a living how you can—same as you say."

"Yes, that's right," said Joss, "and I don't say as there ain't folks as can still get a living off the land. But how do they do that?"

Tod screwed up his face and nodded; but by the look of him, he was evidently thinking of something else.

"Well, some on 'em put all their land to grass," Joss went on, "and farm for milk. Some sell their animals and farm on chemical—I heared of a man as grew five crops of barley running on chemical, all off the same field. And some on 'em grow wheat every other year and fallow in between, and some keep nothen but chickens. All manner of tricks, ain't there, and did you ever see so many farms run to waste or selling ten a penny?"

"Yes, yes," replied Tod perfunctorily; he knew it was no good trying to stop Joss now.

"I don't blame 'em," Joss pressed on, "for trying to get a living, but I tell you, Tod, I can't do that sort of thing. I was brought up to owd-fashioned mixed farming. 'Allus put back as good as you take from the land.' Walter Clary was a good farmer and that was what he larnt me. I must grow crops and I must have animals to stamp my straw. I must muck my land and keep my rotation. I can't do nohow else."

"That's all very fine," said Tod with a grunt, "but that don't pay your tithe."

"I know," said Joss humbly. "I know, but I tell you, Tod, if that warn't for tithe, we could live off the place and make out that way. We can allus grow enow to fill our bellies; but not to pay all them pounds to the Church as well—not with corn at the price that is. What'll they do, d'you reckon, if they take me to court, Tod?"

Tod rubbed his chin and considered. "They might sell up the farm," he said. "More likely they'd take and sell your cows."

Joss felt his features contract, and although Tod's answer was no surprise to him, he looked scared.

"Becourse," continued Tod, "you might join this here tithe-payers' association and then, when they sold the cows, the other members 'd come and buy 'em in cheap, so's they could give 'em back to you. That'd be all right."

"Yes, I know," said Joss, "but 'haps some stranger 'd push in and overbid 'em. There ain't nothen to stop him."

"Yes, 'haps he might," admitted Tod.

"And if they took my cows," continued Joss, "I might as well pack up. They're the only way I can earn a bit of ready money. I durstn't take the risk."

Tod nodded and chewed his lip, thinking hard.

"But what d'you reckon Edgar do?" continued Joss once more. "He ain't the man to give Queen Anne's Bounty all they want."

"If you arst me," said Tod, "I reckon he owe 'em so much he can afford to make 'em an offer, and they're that glad to get some ready cash, they let him off the rest."

"Well, I hain't got the money to make an offer with," said Joss bitterly. "What are the likes of me to do?"

Tod cleared his throat with an air of finality. "I reckon you'll have to have one of these here mortgages," he said. "I can't see nothen else."

"What exactly would that be?" inquired Joss. "I've often heared of such things."

"Why, you get a bloke to lend you the money," Tod explained, "and you pay him the interest. Then if you can't keep on a-paying, they take and sell your farm. That's all honest and lawful," he added, as he caught Joss's dubious look.

"Yes," said Joss, "but I hain't never borrowed money in my life."

" 'Haps not," replied Tod, "but you're about the only farmer as hain't. Most of 'em are up to their eyes in debt."

"Still, I don't like that," protested Joss. "I've allus paid my way. I don't hold with borrowing."

"All right," said Tod, shrugging his shoulders, "you'd better let 'em sell you up then."

"Yes, but what shall I do if I can't pay the interest?" persisted Joss, still struggling with his fate.

"I told you. They'll sell you up," replied Tod inexorably, "but that 'on't be yet. And times may change. Corn may go up and you may make enow to pay the mortgage off. I don't say you 'on't get sold up in the end; but you never know. That might tide you over for a few years."

"I don't like that, I wholly don't," said Joss, shaking his head.

"All right, bor," said Tod, shrugging his shoulders again. "You'd better go to court then; you'll get that over quicker like." He turned his back and began studying the old iron again.

Joss looked round him desperately, but there was no other help in sight; and he could almost feel the policeman's hand on his shoulder.

"I say—I say, Tod," he appealed. "Where could I find a bloke as 'd lend me the money?"

Tod turned round again. "Well, I couldn't tell you," he said, " 'cause I don't hob-nob with that sort; but I know a lawyer in the town as could. He's straight, he is —I do a bit of business with him myself chance-time. He's sure to be in market-day."

"Oh, I see." Joss hesitated, fumbling with his clay pipe. "Let's go and see him now," he said recklessly, and as he spoke the pipe slipped from his fingers to shiver in pieces on the pavement.

Nearly an hour had passed before they were back in the market, and Tod, in case the auctioneer should have begun on the dead stock, was hurrying on.

"God's truth," he exclaimed, as they fetched up by the old iron, "I didn't know I was travelling so fast. I've wholly made you sweat."

Joss smiled uncomfortably. "That warn't the travelling," he said, "but you know, Tod, this here's the first time I ever borrowed a penny in my life. Give me a furrow to plough or a rabbit to catch; but this sort of thing—that's afore my time."

Tod quizzed him over the handle of his walking-stick and then laughed. "I reckon I know what you want," he said, "and there's time enow. The auctioneer ain't halfway through the pigs and he've still got the fowls to do. He 'on't get to the dead-stock sale afore closing-time. That's late o' market-day, remember."

"Yes, I know," said Joss, cheering up a little at the suggestion of a drink. "Trouble is, Tod, I said I'd meet Susy at the fowl sale. She've got some pullets she want me to see put off. They ought to fetch suthun October time, she reckon. Look, here she come, bor. She've seen us already."

"Well, let's all go and have one," said Tod, who was determined to get Joss into a public house without delay, by whatever means. "You can't alter the price of birds by standing there a-garping."

"Hullo, Tod," said Susy, as they strolled up to the fowl-pens to meet her. "Fare to me all Overham's at market to-day. I now seed Edgar taking his wife to the pictures. She's got her fur coat on and that make her stouter than ever, pore thing. But my, that's a queer way to look at anybody," she said, addressing herself to Joss.

"I was thinking," said Joss slowly, and hesitated. "I was thinking," he went on, "you might like to go to the pictures yourself."

Susy stared at him. "Me go to the pictures? Are you talking serious?"

"Yes," said Joss, firmly.

"Well, what made you think that?" demanded Susy.

"Oh, I don't know," replied Joss, again hesitant. "I thought—well, I thought 'haps, all these years, I hadn't given you much chance to enjoy yourself."

Susy stared again. "You ain't crazed, are you?" she said.

"No, I ain't," said Joss, standing his ground. "I mean what I say."

"Oh," said Susy, and her voice had softened. "I didn't mean nothen when I said about Edgar's wife. I don't see no sense in them 'aire pictures. I'd sooner stand in

245

the street and watch the people go by. And not enjoy myself? Why, what d'you reckon I'm a-doing when I take the bread out of the owd oven, or go round the fields a-gathering blackberries for jam; or when I see you eat a good dinner Sundays?"

Joss grinned stupidly and did not answer.

"And when you drive me into market to do a bit of shopping," Susy went on indignantly, "and treat me to a plate of cockles? What d'you take me for, Joss?"

Joss grinned again. "Well, that's all right then," he said.

"What d'you mean?" she asked, puzzled.

"I mean you can keep a-doing all you said," he replied, " 'cause they 'on't turn us out of Chaffinch's now —leastways, not yet awhile."

"No, but—you don't say?" gasped Susy, taken by surprise.

"Yes, I'm borrowing the money," said Joss proudly, "to tide us over—till better times like."

Susy smiled and clapped her hands. "Well, there," she said, "if that ain't a relief! I couldn't bear to leave Chaffinch's, Joss. But who put you up to that?"

Tod, however, whom they had momentarily forgotten, had had enough of the conversation and before Joss could answer, he tapped smartly on his wooden leg with his stick.

"Listen here, together," he said. "If you must go on a-jowing, come along and jow at The Bull."

EDGAR CLARY LAID DOWN "THE FARMER AND STOCK-breeder" and look round his cosy dining-room. On the other side of the fireplace, knitting in the lamplight, sat his wife, vast, solid and necessary, like the Edwardian dining-room furniture; and that, indeed, was how he regarded her, as a piece of furniture. She needed a little polishing, as it were, in the form of regular visits to the pictures and an occasional new dress; but, like the massive sideboard, table and chairs, she performed her function and made no fuss. He had nothing against her.

Further away, at the end of the oblong table, his youngest boy, Arthur, was reading a novel and smoking a cigarette, from which, every minute or so, he carelessly blew a perfect smoke-ring. One of these rings caught Edgar's attention and he glanced sharply at him out of the corner of his eye; for Arthur, who was now nearly eighteen and in his last year at a public school, was one of his principal speculations. A boy at a public school—it was one of those things you naturally invested in as you went up in the world, just like a car or a subscription to the hunt; but although Edgar had duly made the investment, he was not at all satisfied that he was getting his money back. With the other two children it had been so much simpler. Sid was now a partner in his firm of auctioneers and was making money. Irene, in spite of her high-school education, had picked up a Brettsleigh butcher's son at a dance and had married money. Above all they were both common people like himself, with more or less the same ideas, the same ways of talking, the same habits of living; he no longer had much to do with either of them, but he understood and approved of them.

Arthur, on the other hand, whatever else he had learnt at school, and to Edgar most of it was gibberish, Arthur had learnt to be different. He talked like the gentry, with that slightly disdainful tone, natural enough and taken for granted with them, but so disturbing in your own family circle. He always wore plus-fours and stockings while he was home for the holidays, just as if, like the gentry, whose country costume it was, he had nothing to do but play golf or go to shooting parties. He read novels, he was for ever reading novels. He blew smoke-rings; he called dinner "lunch" and supper "dinner"; there was no end to his airs and graces. And then there was that day at Brettsleigh when they had met the master of the hunt in the High Street, and he had talked so glibly about the Winchester match and how School House had won the rackets cup, just as if his parents had not been there, standing on the pavement beside him. The real reason for his being different, and Edgar knew it, was that he wanted to be different. He wanted to be different from his father, because after all his father was nothing more than a common farmer and cattle-dealer, who had not been to a public school and talked like any of his labourers. It was plain that he looked down on his father.

With the same air of careless accomplishment Arthur blew another smoke-ring and Edgar glowered at him. For what right had a bit of a boy like that to look down on him? Edgar was now close on sixty and a Justice of the Peace. He had brought up a family, he had farmed in a big way, he had made money; and apart from the small subvention his wife had brought him at their marriage, he had done it all himself, by his own wits and his own labour. He was a self-made man and as such he felt himself entitled to some respect. It was true that, financially speaking, he was not the man he had been ten years ago; but that was not his fault. Ever since the end of the War things had been going steadily to the bad, and now, in 1932, were worse than they had ever been. What with high wages and low prices, tithe, foot-and-mouth disease and the general depression, it took a shrewd and skilful man to survive at all. But he had survived.

In the first place, even before the end of the War, he had seen what was coming, and on his leasehold farms, where he had lavishly broken grass, he had immediately started farming to leave, taking care to get all he could out of the land and put nothing back. Then, one by one, as the leases expired, he had cleared out of them, until only the six hundred acres of his own property, centring round Foxburrows, were left, and to these he had devoted himself. Here all the meadows were still intact, the arable was in good heart, and every inch could be laid out to save a penny where it could not earn one. Rotations and all the rest of the classic tradition went by the board; for you had to pick up your money where you could, you had to be up to every trick.

As a regular standby, he always grew as much sugar-beet as his arable would carry—there was a government subsidy on it—and by using cheap labour from the town unemployed, he always contrived to make a profit out of it. His other standby was a milking-herd—not too large, for fear of foot-and-mouth—which always brought in ready money; but for the rest he picked up his money, or saved it, where he could. When pigs paid, he was in pigs, when eggs were up, he was in poultry, when beef was up, he was in fat stock; and with his dealer's nose for the market, he always knew the right moment for getting out of whatever he was in. By this elastic system he managed to pay his way, and, what was even more important, to keep his farm in tolerable condition against the time when they would need the farmer again; already he saw another war brewing, clear enough.

However, he still had to live, and this was where his second trade came in. Dealing was certainly not what it had been, but so long as there was any to be done, the dealer was not the one to lose on the gamble; and finally, when, as often happened, there were neither prices nor customers left to gamble with, he still had something to fall back on. His land had made money during the war, but by no means all of it had gone back on the land. Some of it had gone to the Stock

Exchange and was now in Municipal Loans, Banks and Discount Companies, Stores and Catering, Foreign Railways, Mines and Oil, as his newspaper daily reminded him. It brought him in a steady income, which, unlike farming and dealing, had not yet failed him; and it enabled him to maintain his household in comfort. Arthur had no cause to look down on his father.

And yet, in spite of all this, and although the fault was not his, it still remained true that he was not the man he had been. Having a comfortable sufficiency was all very well, but it was not what he had once been used to. It was something very far from the days when he had always been ready to buy another farm, another flock of sheep, another score of beasts, when his name had really counted for something in the district, when life had been an exciting game and one trick had led on to another, bigger trick. Those days might yet return, but not for him, he would be past it then; and meanwhile the game was dull, and the tricks poor little things that added up to nothing. Even this was no reason why Arthur should look down on him, but somehow, when he thought of it, he could not help looking down on himself, and it annoyed him to watch Arthur blowing smoke-rings and reminding him of such things. It made him itch for a chance to assert himself, a chance to prove that this nonsense was untrue; but all he could do was to pour himself out another whisky.

As he did so, the maid tapped at the door and entered.

"If you please, sir," she said, "there's a man want to see you."

"Is that somebody off the farm?" he asked testily; he did not expect his own men to call at the house like that, and at such an hour.

"No, sir," she replied, "that's Mr. Elvin, I believe. He's now waiting in the hall."

Edgar raised his eyebrows and then nodded. "All right," he said, "I'll be there in a minute." He drank up his whisky, frowning and vainly asking himself what Joss's errand could be; but whatever it was, it provided a timely respite from present company.

Joss was waiting for him in the dimly lighted flagged hall with his cap in his hand. It was years since Edgar —at The Rose, most likely—had seen him with his head bare, and he noted how much greyer Joss's dark hair had gone than his own; but unlike him, Joss had no bald patch yet, and the colour in his cheeks was as high as ever.

Joss cleared his throat. "Good evening, Edgar," he said civilly.

"Well, Elvin," said Edgar, as usual resenting and ignoring the familiarity, "what do you want?"

Joss looked at the floor a moment, cleared his throat again, and looked calmly up.

"That's like this here, Edgar," he said. "I've now had an order from the Ministry or suthun. They say I've got to put a concrete floor in my cowshed, and a gutter and all manner of what."

"Yes, I know, we all have," said Edgar. "That's to

make sure the milk don't get tainted, and quite right too."

"Yes, yes, I know," replied Joss, "but trouble is, I can't afford that."

"Well, you'll have to stop keeping o' cows," said Edgar curtly. "That's all."

Joss nodded. "I know," he said, "but—well, if I stop keeping o' cows, I'd better stop farming altogether. What with tithe, you know, and the prices of things—"

"But listen here, Elvin," Edgar interrupted, "what's the good of coming and wasting my time a-telling me that? That ain't my fault."

Joss looked at the floor again and hesitated. "I thought," he said, and then raised his eyes, "I thought 'haps you might want to buy my farm."

Edgar, too, looked at the floor, and then at Joss. The one was as real as the other, but he could not believe his ears.

"Buy your farm?" he echoed.

"Yes," said Joss, "you said you would if you had the chance, more'n once you did."

Confronted with his own words, Edgar instantly became the wary business man. "Ah, yes," he said, "but that was years ago—and besides, what d'you want to sell for?"

"What I told you," replied Joss. "That's the tithe and the bad times, and this here Ministry order on top on 'em—and then there's the mortgage," he added, a little reluctantly.

"A-ah, I reckoned there was suthun else," exclaimed

Edgar, and an involuntary grin of pure satisfaction spread over his face. Joss on his doorstep, begging him to buy Chaffinch's—it was just the thing, that chance to assert himself, that he needed; it made him feel that he counted for something as he had done in the past; it restored his self-esteem. "How much is the mortgage for?" he asked.

"A hundred and ten pounds," said Joss.

"I see, I see," said Edgar, weighing the sum in his mind. "I told you you wouldn't make a do of that, didn't I? You'd have done better by half to work for a master."

Joss gazed at him steadily and did not answer.

"Becourse," continued Edgar, "this ain't the time for anybody to buy farms, nit farmhouses neither."

"Putting you out," Joss interposed, "that ain't only the land I was going to get rid on. I want to keep the house to live in."

Edgar looked at him through narrowed eyelids and laughed. He was thoroughly enjoying himself.

"So that's what you imitated doing?" he said. "Well, what you imitate ain't allus the same as what you can work—not nowadays. Keep the house, eh?"

He laughed again, but Joss maintained his steady, silent gaze.

"Listen here," Edgar went on, "I tell you what I'll do for you, though I reckon I shall suffer for doing that. Still—I'll pay off the mortgage and I'll take the farm, lock, stock and barrel; and you can go on in the house so long as you can pay the rent. That'll be four bob a week."

Joss tightened his lips. "That's a hard bargain," he said.

Edgar shrugged his shoulders. "You can take that or leave that," he said. "Most 'd say I was treating you too kind."

Joss twisted at his cap with both hands and took a deep breath, bracing himself.

"There's another thing," he said quietly. "If I get rid on the farm, I shall have to go out to work. Do you remember the time you told me you'd give forty-five bob for a man like me?"

"Yes, Elvin," said Edgar, shaking his forefinger, "and do you remember when that was? That was years ago, in the middle of the war."

Joss nodded. "But I've got my health and strength," he said. "I can do a day's work with anybody."

Edgar looked him up and down. There was no doubt he could still do with a man as strong and as handy as Joss on the farm, and although it was flattering to his self-esteem to drive a hard bargain, it was still more flattering to be generous—especially, after all his insolence and stubbornness, to be generous to Joss, to make him a dependant; in a word, to get even with him.

"How old are you, Elvin?" he said, when he had finished looking him up and down.

"Let's see, that's April," said Joss. "I was fifty-nine last month."

"Fifty-nine, fifty-nine," repeated Edgar, rubbing his

chin and considering. "I tell you what I'll do, Elvin. If you turn up next Monday, I'll take you on at current labourer's wages—that's twenty-eight bob a week—and you can have the house for four bob. Then as soon as I go to Brettsleigh, I'll get my lawyer to see to the papers. You 'on't only have to sign your name at the bottom. There, I call that treating you handsome."

Joss moistened his lips. "You can't make out without the house?" he said.

"Why, blast, man," replied Edgar, "what's the good of a farm to me without the house? You can't have everything your own way."

"I see," said Joss, in turn rubbing his chin and considering. He knew there was nothing more to be got out of Edgar. "All right," he said at last, "have that as you say, Edgar."

A cold light flickered in Edgar's eyes. "That ain't the way to talk to me," he said.

Joss looked hard at him. "Very well, sir," he said, turning to the door. "I shall be there o' Monday. Good night, sir."

When Joss found himself outside the house again, he was hardly conscious of anything but the cool air and the moonlight, and they had never been more welcome. He breathed deep, and gazed eagerly as the naked black elm-tops took shape around him. For the moment his mind was blank, and the nocturnal world was itself, familiar and acceptable. Then, as he stepped through the garden gate, Susy darted out of the shadow and clutched his arm.

"That's all right, gal," he said, walking her off down the drift. "That's all fixed up, you might say."

He paused, awaiting her approval, her praise, indeed; but instead Susy shook peevishly at his arm.

"Oh, Joss," she scolded, "what ever made you go on so quick? I called you three times arter you went in the gate."

"What?" exclaimed Joss.

"Yes, three times I called you," she repeated, "and you wouldn't listen. I'd have suffered anything afore he should have Chaffinch's. I can't bear that."

"Oh, can't you?" said Joss, much aggrieved and plainly showing it. "Well, you know how you said you couldn't bear to leave Chaffinch's and how glad you were when I said I'd go and see Edgar. That was the only way we could keep the house."

"Yes, yes, I know," she answered ruefully, "but when you went in the gate, I felt different. You a-standing there in front of him and going through all that, and him a-getting what he wanted, just what he've wanted all these years—I couldn't bear that, and I called you back. And then you a-working for him, as ain't fit to black your shoes! Oh, Joss, I'd as soon live in a hole in the ground."

" 'Haps you would," said Joss with a sarcastic sniff, "and 'haps you wouldn't. But you know what I told you afore I went. These here are rum times, with farmers a-standing men off right and left every day. That ain't

257

easy to find a job on the land and the likes of us don't get no dole. How'd you like me working on the roads for fourteen bob a week parish relief? That's all there is for the likes of us. I tell you, my gal, we ought to reckon ourselves lucky. Now then!"

He finished by giving her arm a shake and Susy reluctantly nodded.

"I know you're right," she whimpered, "but blast, if that was anybody but Edgar!"

She began to cry outright and Joss put his arm round her waist to comfort her as they walked along.

"Listen here, gal," he said, "you marn't think about him. We know he'll own the place and all that, but that's us as'll live in the house and farm the garden, like we used to. That was us as made 'em what they are and that's us as'll use 'em now. You might say they'll still be ourn, so far."

"That's right," replied Susy, still struggling with her tears, "and I can still bake in the owd bush-oven. There ain't no bread like that."

"No, there ain't," agreed Joss, "and then, you know, Edgar allus share out his fences among the men, so's to keep the rabbits down, and I reckon he'll let me have my owd 'uns round Chaffinch's so I can allus go out the back door and catch a John when we want one."

"You and your rabbits!" said Susy, with half a smile.

"Yes, yes, gal," Joss pressed on, "and the thing is, we've got twenty-eight bob a week coming in reg'lar every week, and no tithe and no mortgage to pay. We ought to make out easy, and there'll be a shilling or two over, I reckon, for the bus-fare to Brettsleigh and a pint at The Rose. And that ain't all," he added, holding her tighter in his enthusiasm, " 'cause in six years' time we shall be getting ten bob a week from my old-age pension, ten bob a week for nothing. I tell you, gal, I'm glad now I paid my ninepence-for-fourpence money."

Susy nodded, but the ten bob was still a long way off and she had nothing to say for it. Joss, too, for want of response, had come to the end of his flow, and they walked on in silence till the drift came out on the Overham road. Here Joss suddenly stopped.

"I've now remembered," he said. "We must hurry up a bit."

"What ever for?" demanded Susy.

"Why, don't," he replied, "we shan't catch Joe Kerridge's fish-cart."

Susy squeezed his arm appreciatively and this time she laughed.

"I could wholly do with a bit of fish for my supper," she said.

THE IPSWICH FOUR IN HAND DART CLUB WAS PLAYING
its return match with Overham Rose and the taproom there was already full. The members of the two
teams, mostly young men, sat or stood about with their
pint mugs, watching the match, playing games of "fat"
or nap, or just enjoying the perennial pleasure of beer
and conversation in fresh company. A few older men, in
their own more distant way, enjoyed it too. Once, in
their day, when the game was quoits or bowls, they
had been the players; but now they sat back in their
corners, listening contentedly to the hum of voices,
watching the new faces, and exchanging comments.

Among them sat old Joe Kerridge, who had left his
fish-cart outside and dropped in for a wet. Joe was getting on now, as his square white beard showed, and
he had begun to shave his upper lip like a real old man.
He still wore the horsy brown tweeds of his hawking
and dealing days, with their coarse wide stripes, their
ribby raised seams and seven rows of stitching at the
trouser-bottoms; but he no longer fancied himself as a
hawker. It was something to be still on the road with
a horse and trap, but hawking fish was just a regular
round without novelty or excitement, a hard living with

little money and long hours to it. He was tired now at the end of his day and it was already high time to be getting back to his little house at the back of Brettsleigh High Street, where his old lady would be waiting for him with a pot of strong tea and a grilled fresh herring. It was time to be getting back, but even in his old age Joe was a company man, and the warmth and chatter, the sense of something doing, tempted him; another pint would certainly not come amiss. While he was making up his mind, the taproom door opened and in walked Tod Jordan, with what looked like a young sapling under his arm. That settled it.

"Hey, a pint for me and another for my mate," he said, handing his mug to the landlord and then turning to Tod. "How now, bor," he said. "What d'you reckon you're a-doing with that 'aire? A-selling o' clo'esprops?"

Tod grinned in answer and having carefully stowed his burden in a corner behind the door, he came and sat down next to Joe.

"I'll tell you when I've had a wet, bor," he said. "A-getting him up with his roots and then a-lugging him down here—I'm right thirsty, I am. I say, Joe, tidy lot of folks here to-night."

"Yes," said Joe, "that's a dart-match—Ipswich Four in Hand, they tell me. See a bit of life to-night, eh?"

Their two pints arrived and they wished each other good health.

"Now what about this here owd tree?" said Joe, when they had finished wiping their mouths on the backs of their hands.

"Oh, that?" said Tod. "Well, you know young Joss Elvin, I doubt?"

Joe nodded.

"Well, he's sixty-five to-morrow," Tod went on, "and being as he now get his owd-age pension, I've brought him a young walnut to plant in memory like. I didn't get my pension till I was seventy, so I planted one then."

"I reckon you hain't ate no nuts off o' that," said Joe, nudging him.

"Now that's where you're wrong," said Tod, tapping his mug with his forefinger. "You don't know how owd that was when I planted that, and what's more, you don't know how owd I am."

"Talking of age, Tod," said Joe, "how owd are you? I shan't see seventy no more myself."

"Ah," said Tod, with an enigmatic grin, "you'd like to know, wouldn't you? Well, I shan't see seventy again neither."

Joe looked at him doubtfully. "I don't know," he said. "I allus reckoned you was owder'n me, but looking at you, I couldn't say."

Tod grinned again and deliberately changed the subject. "Talking of walnuts," he said, "I allus did like a walnut. I like the nut and I like the tree. The leaves smell nice and that's a master tree to grow fast. But there, I've had a lot to do with 'em in my time. I used to go a-brushing all over this country. Did I ever tell you how I started that?"

"No," said Joe with a grunt; he was not interested in

walnuts. "I didn't know you in those days. You were a young rip, I reckon."

"Well, that's as may be," said Tod, and cocked his head knowingly. "But I'll tell you how I started on the walnut trade. There was an owd bloke about here called Sam Farden, as used to go round a-buying o' walnut-trees autumn time, to sell agin. Well, one night he come into The Rose and he say, 'Is there anybody here can climb a thirty-stave ladder? We're a-brushing to-morrow and there'll be half a sovereign and all the bread and cheese and beer you can get back.' 'All right,' I say, 'I'll have a cut at that.' I warn't only a youngster of eighteen. 'All right, boy,' he say, 'do you meet me at Little Gazing Street seven o'clock time to-morrow.'

"Well, I met him next-day morning and I tell you, I wholly hopped about on that thirty-stave ladder and I throshed and I throshed the owd tree; and the nuts, they came down as thick as raindrops. Then, when that was getting on for dinner-time, I nipped down agin, where owd Sam and his mate were picking up. 'Well,' I say, 'have I kept you busy a-picking up, together?' 'That you have,' said Sam. 'We're half up to our ankles o' nuts.' 'Now do you come and look at the tree,' I say. 'Have I left many behind?' So owd Sam went and had a look, and he say, 'No, boy, you've brushed that well. Here's your half-sovereign and go and get yourself a drink of beer.' Well, that was the start, and arter that I went round a-brushing along o' Sam every autumn for years."

Joe Kerridge looked at Tod's wizened cheeks and little screwed-up eyes, and then at his wooden leg.

"Nobody 'd say so to see you now," he said with a smirk.

"Nobody 'd say you'd been a policeman," retorted Tod, and grinned to see the smirk go off Joe's lip; Joe did not care to be reminded of that episode in his life. "But stand to reason," Tod went on, "that was afore I broke my leg. I tell you, I was right a daring lad. I used to walk right out along the thick owd branches, and when they were too far apart, I used to sling a rope over 'em and shin up; and then chance-time, when you'd been throshing a tidy bit, your knees 'd go all weak. That was the time for a drop of short, and owd Sam Farden allus kept a drop by for me. I could throsh like an owd windmill arter that. And then the beer we used to put down at nights together, with our pockets full of nuts."

He took a drink from his mug and wiped his mouth slowly and thoughtfully. "I was young then," he went on, "and them days a-brushing o' walnuts—I reckon they were the best days of my life. I wholly like an owd walnut-tree."

Joe, now quite serious and attentive, nodded. He understood the quality of Tod's reminiscence and sympathized; it reminded him of his own hawking and dealing days. . . .

There was a shout from the dartboard, where somebody made a lucky shot, and they both looked up.

"Them boys are reg'lar enjoying theirselves," said Tod, "and I don't blame 'em. You're only young once."

264

The door opened and they both turned their heads.

"Why, blast, there's Joss," said Tod, and thumped his empty mug on the table to bring the landlord. "How now, bor?" he said, as Joss nodded and sat down next to him. "I've got a surprise packet here for you to-night."

"Ah?" said Joss, but without any show of interest, or for that matter, even of common friendliness, so hard and unsmiling was his look.

"Three pints, three pints owd," said Tod to the land-lord, who had just picked his way across the crowded room. "We've got a birthday to-day."

He put his hand on Joss's shoulder and pointed to the corner by the door. "There's your surprise packet, bor," he said.

Joss glanced casually at the corner and then back at Tod. "Fare to me like an owd bush," he said ungraciously.

"No, that ain't a bush," Tod explained. "That's a young walnut, and you marn't drink too much to-night; do, you 'on't be able to plant him afore you go to bed. Ah, good, here come the beer. That's so's you 'on't forget the first day of your pension."

"Pension?" Joss glared at him. "Christ, I wish I'd never heared of my bloody pension." He turned his head away, still swearing under his breath.

Tod frowned and paid for the beer. "Now then," he said in his dryest manner, as soon as the landlord was out of hearing, "do you take a sup of that and tell us what wrong we've done. You don't fare over-civil like."

Joss turned back shamefacedly. "I know," he said, "but that 'aire bit about my pension—that was a bit too much. I shan't forget my pension in a hurry."

"What d'you mean?" said Tod.

"Edgar stood me off to-day," said Joss shortly.

Tod's mouth dropped wide open. "Stood you off?" he said.

"Yes," said Joss, "he didn't give me no warning. He just handed me an extra week's wages and said, 'I shan't want you here no more, Elvin. You'll be getting your pension now.' 'But look here, sir,' I say, 'my missis ain't insured and she's a year younger'n me. She 'on't get the pension till she's seventy, and that's another six year. How can we live on ten bob a week, d'you reckon?' 'Ah,' he say, 'you should ha' thought of that afore, Elvin. We've got to give the young 'uns a chance,' and off he went."

The other two stared at him, and then Tod remembered the beer.

"Here, drink up, bor," he said. "No, drink that right up and have another. You wholly want that."

Joss slowly emptied the mug and wiped his mouth. "Yes," he went on bitterly, "ten bob a week and four bob rent to pay. We know there's still a bit left from the valeration and Susy have saved a bit off the chickens; but that 'on't last six year."

"What made him do that?" said Joe Kerridge.

"Well, I've told you what he told me," said Joss, shrugging his shoulders. "He want to give the young 'uns a chance."

266

Tod shook his head and snorted. "That 'on't do, Mr. Clary," he said, "Mr. bloody Clary, J.P. Why, they can't get the young 'uns to go on the land nowadays to larn the trade; and a man like Joss, do you tell me how many young 'uns he's worth. No, you've got to look furder'n that, together."

He caught the landlord's eye and pushed Joss's empty mug across the table. "Fill that up agin, please," he said, "and put in a drop of gin."

"Well," said Joss with a judicial air, "we all know he wanted the little owd farm. He didn't want that to farm hisself, becourse, 'cause a few years more, and that 'll be as bad as when I first came; properly let go, that is. No, he just wanted Chaffinch's for his'n, and he got what he wanted. But standing me off—what do he get out of that? He warn't a bad master, I will say, and we never had what you might call a wry word. What do he get out of that, I want to know?"

"Well, do you want to know?" said Tod, thrusting his face forward at Joss. " 'Cause I'll tell you. Edgar'd got a down on you and he wanted to work that off. He'd got that all planned out, I tell you. D'you remember how, when he took you on, he arst you how owd you were? You told me yourself."

Joss nodded. "I doubt you're right," he said, " 'cause Susy say just the same. I don't know what we're to do," he added despairingly.

"I'll tell you what to do," said Tod, as the mug of gin and beer was set down on the table. "Do you get that back and cheer yourself up a bit."

He pushed the mug across to Joss and watched him drink a mouthful.

"Now I'll tell you, together, what I think," he went on indignantly. "That's a dirty rotten trick, what Edgar 've done, but that ain't wholly a surprise to me, 'cause I never did like the bastard. But I reckon there's suthun worse."

He paused to take a sip at his beer and wipe the sweat off his forehead; he was quite red in the face with indignation.

"Yes," he went on, raising his voice as if he wanted the whole room to hear, "and I'll tell you what that is. Here's Joss, he's sixty-five to-day and a gret big strong feller—he'll be good till he's nearly eighty. And Joss wholly know how to farm—you remember, that was him and not Edgar they wanted on the Trust Farm years ago. There ain't a better farmer—not to speak of farming—in the whole parish. But will they let him farm? 'No, you shall work for a master,' they say. So Joss work for a master, work like a bloody hoss, he do. And then they 'on't let him work no more. 'You're out of date, you shall go on the pension,' they say. So Joss go on the pension, but they 'on't give him and his missis enow to live on. Yes, and here we are in nineteen thirty-eight, in a free and Christian country, and the papers all a-telling us there's another war a-coming and we must grow more food. Don't you call that a bloody scandal, together, to treat a good man like that?"

Tod was so indignant that he was now addressing the

company at large, but the company at large, having come to the end of its dart-match, was now embarked on the chorus of *Roll Along, Covered Waggon*, and paid him no more attention than any other single voice in the general hubbub. Even Joss, yielding to his gin and beer, had begun to forget his troubles and was drumming his fingers in time to the music.

"I do like an owd singsong," he said with a grin.

Tod stopped short and mopped his face again. Joss, at least, he thought, might have listened to him, but he was not annoyed; to keep Joss's mind on what had happened was the last thing he wanted.

"I'm glad you're feeling better, bor," he said. "We're going to have a song from you to-night."

"No, no," said Joss hastily. "I ain't in the mind to-night."

But Tod was not to be denied. The chorus had now given way to the quieter hubbub of talk, and Tod rose with his mug in his hand.

"Order, gentlemen," he cried, "order, gentlemen, please."

The young men glanced round at him; but they still went on talking.

"No, no, Tod," repeated Joss, frowning and shaking his head, "that's right a long time since I last sung a song. I ain't in the mind, I tell you."

"You soon will be, once you've started," answered Tod relentlessly. "Order, gentlemen, please. Mr. Joss Elvin will now sing that good owd ditty, *The Young Sailor Cut Down in His Prime*."

"Yes, come along, Joss," added Joe Kerridge. "That's a good song, that is. You sing that well."

The beer, the warmth and the company had already gone a long way with Joss; and Joe Kerridge's insistence completed their work. It was Joe who had first set him off singing.

"All right," he said, grinning and dragging himself to his feet, "I'll sing for you, together."

"Order, gentlemen, please," cried Tod again, but the young men still went on talking.

Joss, however, did not wait for order. He was used to imposing his voice on noisy, indifferent company, and once you had got them into the first chorus, they were no more trouble. He lifted up his chin, took a breath, and started right off on the first verse.

One day as I strolled along by The Royal Albion,
Dark was the morning and bitter the day.

His voice was no longer so strong and ringing as once it had been; but he could still sing in tune, and above all he knew his song, every note and every word of it, off by heart.

Who should I spy but one of my shipmates,
Wrapped in a blanket far colder than clay?
He called for a candle to light him to bed with,
Also a blanket to wrap round his head.
His poor head was aching, his poor heart was breaking,
For he was a young sailor cut down in his prime.

The young men still went on talking, but let them talk; they would see now.

"Now then, all together, boys—" He raised his mug and beat time with it to set them going.

So we will beat the drums over him and play the fifes
    merrily,
Play the dead march as we carry him along.

But the young men still talked, they hardly seemed aware that any one was singing; and the only other sound in the room came from three cracked voices, Tod's, Joe's and his own, struggling on alone with the chorus.

We will take him to the churchyard and fire three vol-
    leys over him,
For he was a young sailor cut down in his prime.

As they struggled on to the end, a piano was trundled in from the bar parlour and the din became greater.

Tod leapt to his feet again.

"Order, order!" he cried. "Give 'em the second verse, Joss. We'll larn 'em, the young bastards."

Joss badly wanted to sit down. It was no pleasure singing to those who would not listen, and, he knew it now, his voice was as cracked as the other two; but with Tod backing him up like that, he had to go on.

His poor aged father, his good old mother,
Often have told him about his past life.

Along with those flash girls his money he squandered,
Along with those flash girls he took his delight.

In the middle of the verse the piano slid home with a crash under the dartboard, and Tod leapt up yet again, calling for order. Joss, his solitary voice sounding more cracked than ever, hastened on.

But now he is dead and laid in his coffin,
Six jolly sailor-boys walk by his side.
Each of them carried a bunch of white roses,
So every one might smell them as we passed by.

He was all in a sweat when he got to the end, but once more he raised his mug hopefully:
"Now then, all together, boys—"
At the same moment as he raised his mug, the piano struck up, and it was followed by a sudden burst of song that seemed to sweep him off his feet.

If you were the only girl in the world
And I were the only boy—

The whole room was singing it.
That finished him. It was bad enough getting the sack from Edgar; but being bawled down like this, in the middle of his favourite song, was even worse; for it proved, what nothing else had proved, that he was really out of date, out of date and unwanted. He did not wait for more, but sank down on his seat and took refuge in his mug.

Tod, however, had not yet given up the fight. He was up on his feet again at once, redder in the face than ever.

"You young bastards," he cried, "don't you know a good song when you hear one? A good song and a good singer?"

Several of the company turned round and laughed. It was the first time they had taken any real notice of Tod and his friends.

"See those three owd codgers?" said one of the town visitors to his neighbour. "There's three owd-timers for you."

Joss overheard him and glanced at his two companions. Tod in his velvet "frock" and "pheasant" cords, Joe Kerridge with his shaven upper lip above his white beard and his horsy dealer's clothes, himself in his corduroy sleeved waistcoat buttoned up to the neck and his heavy corduroy over-jacket; they were old-timers among all these youngsters in their city reach-me-downs. "Three owd codgers," in fact.

"Don't be a fool, Tod," he growled. "Set down, for God's sake, do."

"Yes, set down, Tod," said Joe.

But Tod was not to be ruled by any one. "You young bastards," he cried again, "don't you know behaviours?"

"Here, that'll do, Tod."

Together, Joss and Joe Kerridge seized his arms, and since Tod was a heavy old man, they used considerable force. But to their surprise, there was no resistance. He seemed to collapse like a heap of chaff, and before they

273

were quite aware what was happening, he had slid down under the table.

"God's truth," gasped Joss, "I didn't know he was as drunk as that."

Joe Kerridge, however, had already pushed the table back and was down on his knees beside him.

"Drunk?" he said, as he fumbled with Tod's neckerchief. "Do you just take a look at his jaw. They larnt me all about that in the police."

By this time both dart-teams had properly taken notice and were crowding round the table to stare. Joe Kerridge looked sourly up at them.

"Somebody go and fetch a doctor," he said. "That's a stroke."

CHAPTER TWENTY

March 1938

THE THREE-ACRE MEADOW WHERE TOD JORDAN'S CARA-
van stood was almost in the parish of Little Gazing. It
was surrounded by a thick hawthorn hedge, for years
uncut, and in keeping with Tod's original trade of
woodman, it backed upon a little strip of copse.

"Well, fancy that!" said Susy, as Joss unfastened the
gate. "I reckon I've been this way half a dozen times
and I never knowed Tod's place was here."

With difficulty Joss heaved the gate open a foot or
two and they passed through.

"Well, yes," he replied, "that was just Tod all over.
There warn't a better company man in the county of
Suffolk, but at home he somehow kept hisself to hisself. Becourse, chance-time a stranger 'd look in in the
way of business—come to that, I've been here several
times myself; but he'd never arst you into the caravan
and he never left the door open so's you could see inside. I reckon that was along o' being a sort of travelling bloke. He was a bit independent like. Same as his
age. Nobody knowed he was nearly eighty-two till he
died."

"Ah, that's a great age," said Susy sententiously, as
she picked her way through the wet grass.

"Yes, and he was good for several year more," added Joss, "if he hadn't gone to that dart-match and excited hisself."

"H'm, I ain't sure," said Susy acidly, "—living in an owd place such as this. Is that the caravan?"

She pointed to a corner of the meadow against the copse, where a glass-panelled door, a pair of shafts and a pair of low wheels were just visible between two towering mounds of bramble.

"Yes, that's the place," said Joss, trying his best not to sound apologetic. "I reckon Tod didn't want nobody to know where he lived at all."

Susy sniffed. "If you arst me," she said, "he lived wholly damp in the middle of them owd bushes."

Joss glanced anxiously at her; that was just what he had been afraid she would say.

"Still that hain't allus got to stand there," he replied diplomatically.

Susy did not answer, but her mouth looked prim and mistrustful.

"What's all these chips under foot?" she said, as they walked up to the steps of the caravan.

"Why, that belong to his wood-cutting days," said Joss, "but that was years ago."

Susy sniffed again. "Well, he'd had plenty of time to sweep that up," she said, and then paused to look critically at Tod's former habitation.

"That ain't right a caravan," she said at last. "That's more like an owd shepherd's hut on wheels."

"Yes, that is," Joss agreed, "but that's bigger'n most,

and I reckon that 'on't be like a shepherd's hut inside."

"Well, that wholly want a coat of paint outside," retorted Susy. "Have you got the key?"

Joss had the key all ready and thrust it in the keyhole, but somehow, in his nervousness, he could not get it to turn.

"Here, come along, do," said Susy, elbowing him out of the way, and with one twist of her fingers she had the door wide open. "Well, there!" she exclaimed.

The first thing that met her eyes, as she peered into the dim interior, was a small mahogany table in the middle with a red plush tablecloth on it. On either side of this were two full-length bunks, also of mahogany, and fitted underneath with drawers of various sizes. One of them was upholstered in red plush to match the tablecloth. The other was draped with an ornate crimson coverlet, in the middle of which a silk-embroidered peacock spread his plumes. Further in, beyond the table and the bunks, it was just possible to discern a tiny iron grate, complete with fender, oven, mantelshelf and copper kettle, and on one side of it a glass-doored cupboard displaying Tod's crockery. Susy stepped up into the van, gazing in wonder around her, and as he followed her, Joss struck a match. Susy gasped aloud.

"Oh, look, Joss," she cried, "do you look at that stove and that copper kittle, how they shine. They might just have been polished this morning, and that brass lamp on the ceiling too."

"Yes, and look at his one Sunday boot," said Joss, pointing under the table. "That's fit to go to church in."

Susy nodded and ran her hands over the woodwork of the bunks. "And not a speck of dust nowhere," she said, "though that's a week since he was last here. I never reckoned Tod 'd have things as smart as this."

Joss put his head on one side. "I don't know," he said thoughtfully. "Tod was allus partic'ler about his clo'es. You remember his velvet frock and pheasant cords?"

Susy nodded again and quite reverently lifted the end of the crimson coverlet.

"Ain't this beautiful?" she said, "and look, Joss, there's real lace on the pillows. Well, I never did. Real lace!"

Joss bent over and admired. "D'you know," he said, "I reckon Tod had them things from his missis what died. She was a gyppo, you see, and gyppos like things smart when they can get 'em. I reckon he kept all that up along of her."

" 'Haps he did," said Susy, still gazing round her in wonder. "But there, you could knock me down with a feather."

"I don't see no sign of mould," suggested Joss cautiously.

Susy shook her head. "No, no," she said, smoothing a pillow with her hand; "that's as dry as a bone."

"Well, now do you come and have a look outside," said Joss, and led the way down the steps and across to a small, open-fronted building with a thatched roof. "This here used to be Tod's workshop, I remember that, where he made his hurdles and rakes and clo'es-props. Look, there's the copper where he used to boil his walking-sticks."

278

"That'd take a tidy lot of linen," said Susy approvingly.

"And look at all his tools," continued Joss, leading her round and watching her closely. "Did you ever see such a lot of owd hooks and saws and axes?"

"There's some dust here," remarked Susy, poking her finger down an axe-helve.

"Ah, well," said Joss deprecatingly, "he give that trade up years ago. But do you look here." He picked up a billhook from the chopping-block and smiled as he ran his finger along its shining edge. "Trust Tod to keep the hook he used sharp," he said. "That's the one he chopped his kindling with, I doubt."

"What's that door there?" said Susy, pointing to a corner of the workshop.

"That's the stable," said Joss, "but ever since the night Tod died, the pony have been down at The Rose, and the trap too. We can look at them on the way back. I want you to take a peek behind here now." He hurried her round to the back of the stable, where he stopped and pointed. "There," he said proudly, "that's Tod's owd iron."

It stretched fully fifty yards along the hedge, a regular museum of old iron. There were farm implements of all kinds, from ploughs to self-binders, in various stages of dissolution. There were bedsteads, bicycles, fenders, saucepans, gramophones, sewing machines, motorcars and even a traction engine. There were heaps of rusty chains, of nuts and bolts, of old tin cans. There was almost everything made of iron that you could think of.

Susy stood still, taking it all in, and then turned slowly round, to take in the stable and workshop, the caravan and the rest of the meadow, as well.

"Do all this belong to us?" she asked, with something very near awe in her look.

Joss nodded solemnly. "That's what the will say," he replied. "Tod left us everything he'd got, owd iron and all. And he had the lawyer put in a bit about the goodwill of the business and write out a list of the folks he bought of and sold to. I tell you, Tod didn't forget nothen."

"Yes, but is there anything in that?" said Susy, still a little mistrustful. "In owd iron, I mean?"

"Well, Tod made a living out of that," said Joss, scratching his head, "and he never stinted hisself o' nothen, you might say. Not to the last, he didn't. And now I remember a thing he told me, not long afore he died. 'There's going to be money in that arter I'm finished,' he said, ' 'cause there's another war a-coming and they'll want that 'aire stuff for guns and all manner of what.' That's what he said."

"Well, there," said Susy, turning to view the old iron once more and plainly impressed, "pore Tod have been a good friend to us."

"He wholly have," said Joss, and then collected himself; the moment, he judged, was ripe. "Listen here, gal," he said, tapping her on the shoulder, "do you reckon you could live in a little owd van like a gyppo?"

Susy turned round and faced him. "What, a nice little place like that?" she said. "I wholly could. I ain't proud.

But"—she smiled mockingly at him—"what about you? You've allus had your comforts, a reg'lar house and garden like."

Joss laughed, he felt so relieved. "I shan't take no harm," he said, "don't you worry. Besides, this here bit of ground where Tod used to grow his taters—I shall make that into a proper garden, and that owd workshop of Tod's 'd just do for half a dozen store pigs; and then there's another thing. Tod was no farmer, you might say, but I reckon I could put down half the midder to suthun, oats or beans or clover. That 'd come in handy for the owd pony; and chance-time we could have a bit of wheat for weselves—'cause, well, first thing I do, I must build an owd bake-oven for you under the shed."

Susy giggled and nudged him with her elbow. "There you go," she said. "Just like Chaffinch's all over agin. You've got all that planned out, hain't you?"

Joss, however, suddenly looked serious. "Becourse, that's all right for me," he said, "but there's suthun I'd forgot. I'd forgot your rheumatics."

Susy shook her head. "You needn't worry," she said reassuringly. "They 'on't hurt in there. That little owd van's as dry as a bone, I tell you. And here's another thing, Joss." She laid her hand on his arm and her face became as serious as his. "Even if that warn't, I'd put up with the rheumatics to have our own place and be our own masters."

Joss grinned contentedly and then, surveying his new property, he began to whistle.

"What's that tune you're whistling?" said Susy, shaking his sleeve.

Joss grinned again and in a rather cracked, half-falsetto voice, he began to sing:

There was an owd couple and they were pore,
Lived in a house with only one door.
Oh, what a pore couple were they!

Lightning Source UK Ltd.
Milton Keynes UK
UKHW01f1055280818
327913UK00001B/62/P